AFRICAN ISSUES

Series Editors Alex de Waal & Stephen Ellis

Fighting 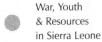 War, Youth
for the & Resources
Rain Forest in Sierra Leone

PAUL RICHARDS

The Lie Challenging
of the Received Wisdom on the
Land African Environment

Edited by

MELISSA LEACH & ROBIN MEARNS

Peace How the IMF
without Blocks Rebuilding
Profit in Mozambique

JOSEPH HANLON

Famine Politics & the
Crimes Disaster Relief Industry
in Africa

ALEX DE WAAL

The Criminalization
of the State
in Africa

JEAN-FRANÇOIS BAYART, STEPHEN ELLIS
& BÉATRICE HIBOU

Africa Disorder
Works as Political
Instrument

PATRICK CHABAL & JEAN-PASCAL DALOZ

AFRICAN ISSUES

Africa Works Disorder as Political Instrument

Africa Works

Disorder as Political Instrument

PATRICK CHABAL
King's College, London

JEAN-PASCAL DALOZ
CNRS, Centre d'Etude
d'Afrique Noire, Bordeaux

The International
African Institute

in association with

JAMES CURREY
Oxford

INDIANA UNIVERSITY PRESS
Bloomington & Indianapolis

The International
African Institute
in association with

James Currey
73 Botley Road
Oxford OX2 0BS
&
Indiana University Press
601 North Morton Street
Bloomington
Indiana 47404
(North America)

British Library Cataloguing in Publication Data

Chabal, Patrick
  Africa works : disorder as political instrument. - (African issues)
  1.Africa - Politics and government - 1960 -
  I.Title II.Daloz, Jean-Pascal
  320.9'6

ISBN 0-85255-819-8 (James Currey Cloth)
ISBN 0-85255-814-7 (James Currey Paper)

Library of Congress Cataloging-in-Publication Data
A catalog record for this book is available from the Library of Congress

ISBN 0-253-21287-1 (paper)
ISBN 0-253-33525-6 (cloth)

Typeset by
Saxon Graphics Ltd, Derby
in 9/11 Melior with Optima display

Printed in Great Britain by
Villiers Publications
London N3

To Farzana
&
Wendy-Anne

CONTENTS

ACKNOWLEDGEMENTS

This book is the outcome of a particularly auspicious collaboration between two scholars issuing from different backgrounds but sharing the same intellectual outlook on the political analysis of Black Africa. We wish to record here that working together has been both pleasant and enlightening.

This book would not have been possible without the friendly and academic support of a number of colleagues, of whom we want to mention Paul Richards, Murray Last, John Peel, Jean-François Médard, Daniel Bach, Daniel Bourmaud, Henri Ossébi, Richard Sklar, Crawford Young, Michael Schatzberg, Thomas Callaghy, Richard Joseph, Peter Schraeder and C. D. Halisi. We want to thank most particularly Farzana Shaikh for her careful and thoughtful editing of the entire book and Lesley Daloz for her continuous assistance. We acknowledge the support of our respective institutions, King's College London and the CEAN. Finally, we would like to register our debt to Alex de Waal for having encouraged us to publish our work in the IAI African Issues series and to Douglas H. Johnson for ensuring that the book was published quickly.

London & Bordeaux

NOTE ON THE AUTHORS

Patrick Chabal is Professor of Lusophone African Studies, King's College, University of London. He has lived and worked in Cameroon and done research in Guinea–Bissau, Senegal, Cape Verde, Lesotho, Mozambique and South Africa. He has written a large number of articles on the history, politics and literature of Africa, with particular reference to the Portuguese-speaking countries. He is the author of many books, including *Amilcar Cabral: revolutionary leadership and people's war* (Cambridge University Press, 1983); *Power in Africa: an essay in political interpretation* (Macmillan, 1992 and 1994); and *The Postcolonial Literature of Lusophone Africa* (C. Hurst, Northwestern University Press, Witwatersrand University Press, 1996). He is the editor of *Political Domination in Africa: reflections on the limits of power* (Cambridge University Press, 1986).

Jean-Pascal Daloz is Senior Researcher of the Centre National de la Recherche Scientifique, based at the Institut d'Etudes Politiques de Bordeaux, Centre d'Etude d'Afrique Noire. He was founder of the French Research Institute (IFRA) in Nigeria at the University of Ibadan, and Director of the French Research Institute for the southern Africa area, at Harare, Zimbabwe. He is the author of *Société et politique au Nigéria* (Institut d'Etudes Politiques de Bordeaux, 1992), and a co-editor of several books including *Paris, Pretoria and the African Continent: the international relations of states and societies in transition* (Macmillan and St Martin's Press, 1996), and *Transitions démocratiques africaines: dynamiques et contraintes* (Karthala, 1997).

Introduction ▮ The Question of Analysis

This book is an attempt to make sense of what is happening in Africa today. Simple as this aim may appear to be, it is in fact fiendishly challenging for reasons having to do with both the diversity of the continent and the complexity of the events currently taking place there. How, for example, can we hope to explain in a single volume the present crisis of the Great Lakes region, the civil wars in Sudan, Liberia and Angola, as well as the widespread failure of development in most African countries. Is our undertaking over-ambitious? Should it even be attempted? Would the level of generalization required to account for such intricate and diverse experiences reduce the validity of any of the observations we might make?

We would argue, however, that it is the depth and seriousness of the present African crisis which make our enterprise necessary. Furthermore, our undertaking is not so bold as to assume that one book could provide the key to an understanding of the contemporary history of so many different countries. Such is in any case not our intention. We seek instead to provide the analytical framework, the instruments, which we believe can help explain the condition of contemporary Africa. Even so, the task is daunting and there is no gainsaying the difficulty of developing a conceptual perspective which can serve a recognizably useful purpose in the present interpretative confusion over the African predicament.

As we shall have cause to explain throughout our book, the acuteness of Africa's crisis is such as to defy the usual parameters of current political analysis. Much of what is written (by journalists or 'experts') on current events in Africa, including the prospects for democracy, reads like a litany of well-worn clichés about the (dark) continent. Clichés are always the resort of the analytically feeble, but they are not always wrong, based as they are on some distorted perception of actual events, on some kernel of truth, and that is why they deserve to be taken seriously, even (or particularly) by scholars.

In the present circumstances of Africa, then, the challenge facing political analysis is to elucidate what is difficult to comprehend, to make sense of what appears senseless or arbitrary, and to meet the clichés head-on. This inevitably involves a degree of generalization about events and people and a comparison of what might at first appear not amenable to comparison. It is to privilege the analytical over the monographic. That is why our book is not designed as a reference volume about the contemporary political situation in Africa; nor even as a compendium of what makes the African crisis so acute. It is, instead, a discussion of what we regard as some of the key issues in Black Africa today.

It is, however, an attempt to enhance the political analysis of the continent from a perspective which is intelligible to the non-political scientist. Although we would see ourselves as working within the tradition of 'classical' (as opposed to merely 'area studies') political analysis, it is one of our main ambitions to reach out beyond the narrow confines of academe to any reader interested in contemporary Africa. Indeed, we subscribe to the view that the relevance of political analysis is very largely to be measured by the extent to which it sheds new light on events hitherto only poorly understood.

We shall not rehearse here in detail the elements of the African crisis, as most of them are familiar enough to those who follow current events: the failure of economic development, political instability, societal divisions, violence, crime and civil war. Neither shall we focus on the difficulties involved in interpreting this crisis from the post-colonial perspective of our Western societies.[1] Nor, finally, shall we join the current political debate about the prospects for democratization in Africa. Although present political transitions in Africa are important, and the desirability of democracy is in principle not to be denied, an assessment of the prospects for greater democracy demands that we approach the task of explaining contemporary African politics from a different analytical angle.

We intend in this Introduction to outline our argument and the framework which we employ. We present first the premises on which our analysis is constructed. We then discuss briefly some of the book's main arguments.

Ours is a five-dimensional approach. First, we stress the importance of actual events. Our inquiry starts from the empirical observation of present-day realities and not from any preconceived notion of what

---

[1] For a systematic discussion of our (Western) perceptions of the current African crisis, see Chabal, 1996.

ought or ought not to be analysed. We cannot, for example, decide *a priori* that certain forms of African politics (e.g., the genocide in Rwanda, the disintegration of Zaire, or the smooth democratic transition in Cape Verde) are temporary aberrations which are not representative of existing trends on the continent. We need to attempt to explain what is actually happening on the ground in Africa, however unpalatable it may be.

Second, we use universal analytical tools, rather than Africa-specific conceptual instruments. What we mean concretely is that our framework meets the same criteria of explanatory rigour and validity as used for the analysis of our own societies. We assume, for instance, that political action in Africa can be explained in terms of rational behaviour, not merely 'backwardness'. Africans do not behave any less, or any more, rationally than anyone else. The task for analysis is to explain such rationality in terms which lend themselves to the demands of political (and, in particular, comparative) analysis.

Third, our approach is multi-disciplinary – for the simple, but overwhelmingly powerful, reason that the reality of politics in contemporary Africa is exceptionally multi-faceted. Whilst, in the West, the realm of politics is relatively well-defined and self-contained, both concretely and analytically separate from those, for instance, of the economy or society, such is emphatically not the case in Africa. To confine our inquiry to those areas which in classical political analysis constitute what might be called formal politics would be to limit our analysis to the world of shadows. Understanding politics in Africa is understanding how Africans experience and live politics in their daily existence, and such today is the intricacy of that political experience that we need to be catholic in our method.

Fourth, our method is comparative, in that it seeks to provide an analysis of politics which integrates the experience of contemporary Africa with the rest of the world. One test of the quality of political analysis is that it should be readily understandable by those who are not familiar with the particularities of the countries under study. This requires that we make it easier to compare similar events in Africa and elsewhere. An explanation of the conflict in Liberia, for example, must make sense of what is happening without resorting to the so-called mysteries of Africa's 'barbarism'. Or rather, the 'barbarism' of the occurrences in Liberia, like that of the former Yugoslavia, must be explained without resorting to facile *sui generis* (culture-bound and often racist) explanations. It is the task of the analyst to explain, not rant.

Fifth, our inquiry is historical – in two complementary ways. On the one hand, we try to explain processes in their proper historical context. On the other hand, we seek to ground our analysis in an understanding of the historical continuities – the deep history – which we know to be of importance in the comprehension of our own societies. This is crucial, for it seems to be the enduring fate of Africa to be 'explained' in terms which are so ahistorical as to be risible -- a lowering of analytical standards which we would reject out of hand if it were applied to the societies in which we, in the West, live. Would we, for instance, explain the conflict in Northern Ireland solely in terms of 'ancestral tribal hatreds' or political scandals in France exclusively in terms of 'the politics of the belly'?

To speak of transitions is to understand continuities in their historicity. To study causalities is to make sense of the movement of societies over time. An historical approach, then, is one which attempts to explain events in contemporary Africa within the long span which connects the present to the pre-colonial past. What we mean can be expressed in two connected propositions: (1) the present-day crisis, or more broadly disorder, in Africa is a crisis of modernity, and (2) this crisis of modernity is rooted in the deep history of the societies in which it is taking place.

The aim of our book, therefore, is clear although some of its conclusions may not be fashionable. We do not start from the premise that there is currently in Africa a trend towards democratization or, even, that present transitions are for the better. Ours is purely an analytical approach, not a prescriptive or normative one. We do not seek to pass judgement on what is happening, either positively or negatively, other than to deplore poverty and lament human rights abuses. As Africanists, we believe strongly that what we are best placed to do is to refine the analysis of contemporary political processes in Africa.[2] What we have to say may, at times, be controversial but we say it in the constructive spirit which all debate should generate, and from the perspective of two scholars who have lived, worked and regularly done research in Africa for the best part of the last two decades.

The paradigm for our analysis – which we develop in full at the end of the book – is what we call the political instrumentalization of disorder. In brief, it refers to the process by which political actors in Africa seek to maximize their returns on the state of confusion, uncertainty, and sometimes even chaos, which characterizes most African polities.

---

[2] Our responsibility lies in being as critical in our analysis as we would be in the analysis of our own societies. The most grievous mistake we could make, which would also be the worst betrayal of our commitment to Africans, would be to lessen the critical quality of our analysis on the spurious grounds of political correctness. The time has long passed when we, Westerners, had to expiate the colonial crimes of our forefathers. We need to engage in constructive dialogue with our African colleagues, openly and on level ground, with only one design in mind: to contribute to a better understanding of Africa.

Although there are obviously vast differences between countries in this respect, we would argue that what all African states share is a generalized system of patrimonialism and an acute degree of apparent disorder, as evidenced by a high level of governmental and administrative inefficiency, a lack of institutionalization, a general disregard for the rules of the formal political and economic sectors, and a universal resort to personal(ized) and vertical solutions to societal problems.

To understand politics in such a context is to understand the ways in which individuals, groups and communities seek to instrumentalize the resources which they command within this general political economy of disorder. To speak of disorder is not, of course, to speak of irrationality. It is merely to make explicit the observation that political action operates rationally, but largely in the realm of the informal, uncodified and unpoliced – that is, in a world that is not ordered in the sense in which we usually take our own polities in the West to be.[3]

In a world of disorder there is a premium both on the vertical and personalized infra-institutional relations through which the 'business' of politics can be conducted and on access to the means of maximizing the returns which the 'domestication' of such disorder requires. To give two examples: where foreign aid is available, it is profitable to exploit any connection with those who control the 'distribution' of such aid. Similarly, access to the officials who oversee trade flows through international or even internal borders is necessary in order to maximize their return on the disorder generated by the apparent arbitrariness in the permeability of those borders.

What we mean here is that the notion of disorder should not be construed, as it normally is in classical political analysis, merely as a state of dereliction. It should also be seen as a condition which offers opportunities for those who know how to play that system. Whether, however, such a situation is conducive to (economic and political) development as it is normally understood is a totally different question – and one to which we shall return at the end of the book. We are here simply concerned to provide an analysis of what we observe in contemporary Africa. If, as we believe, there prevails in Africa a state of generalized disorder, as defined above, then it behoves us to explain how such disorder is instrumentalized politically.

Disorder also incorporates within it the notion of uncertainty, a concept with which economists are familiar. Once more, uncertainty is both a cost and an opportunity, against which there is a premium. In a polity of disorder, the ability to hedge uncertainty is a valuable resource – hence, the perennial significance which witchcraft retains

---

[3] In an ordered, regulated polity, political opportunities and resources are defined explicitly and codified by legislation or precedent.

as an almighty hedge in Africa. Knowledge and the control of information are important in all polities but they are critical in disordered societies, where they impinge even more critically on the management of uncertainty. Whether, for example, the ruler is unwell, or prey to new (perhaps occult) influences, will be of substantially greater significance in Africa than it would be in Europe, for it could unleash a wholesale change in the patrimonial networks extant and radically reshape the existing moral economy of disorder.

In sum, then, the connecting thread between the arguments presented in the following nine chapters is that the analysis of contemporary African politics requires sustained attention to the intricacies of the ways in which the present crisis of modernity in Africa appears to be worked through the instrumentalization of disorder. We are, of course, aware that our emphasis on disorder may prompt ideologically motivated or intellectually torpid readers to draw unwarranted normative conclusions about Africa and Africans. This is a danger that is impossible to avoid since such interpretations are driven by the need to belittle Africa and demean Africans – a need as powerful as that which fuels racism in our own countries. To desist because of such a danger would be a dereliction of our responsibility as Africanist scholars.

We would point out, however, that the motivation for our book lies partly with our impatience with existing intellectual sloth in respect of Africa, sloth which itself has been widely exploited by those who seek to diminish Africans. We would also warn that our book will give little succour to the reductionist since it makes clear that what is happening in Africa is in no way unique. Much of what we discuss has already happened elsewhere in the world in earlier periods and could well happen again in those parts of the world which now view Africa with such distaste – as the ghastly recent history of the break-up of Yugoslavia makes perfectly plain.

Our book is divided into four parts. The first is explicitly concerned with the sphere of politics: the state, civil society and political elites. We would argue that in Africa the unofficial has always been more significant than the official but that the present crisis, which has led to a severe reduction in existing resources, is contributing to a growing trend towards the informalization of politics. We show here how the African political systems are only superficially akin to those of the West (in terms of their institutions, constitutions and the rule of law). In reality, it is the patrimonial and infra-institutional ways in which power is legitimated which continue to be politically most significant.

The second part broadens the picture and looks at politics from a cultural perspective, examining in some detail the extent to which the issue of identity, the domain of religious beliefs and the pervasive climate of violence impinge on society. Our aim here is to stress how the dynamics of African modernization are compatible with what we in the West tend to regard as 'traditional' characteristics. The key question here, therefore, is less that of the cultural influences suffered by the continent than that of its 're-traditionalization'.

The third section, entitled somewhat provocatively, 'the productivity of economic failure', is meant to reassess a number of important economic issues relevant to the understanding of the present crisis on the continent. We aim here to explain why corruption is the norm, to analyse the ways in which dependence may constitute a substantial resource, and to show how it is possible for Africans to enrich themselves whilst the continent is failing to develop.

Throughout the nine chapters of the book we make every effort to furnish the analytical and empirical evidence for our approach. In the fourth, and final, part, we present a systematic development of our paradigm – the political instrumentalization of disorder. Our intention is not to elaborate an all-embracing theoretical model. The time for grand synthesis of this type is long gone. We aim instead to offer a sufficiently reasoned and detailed exposition of our paradigm to generate a more focused and fruitful discussion about contemporary Africa.

* * * *

We enter two important caveats: the first on the scope of our inquiry; the second on the structure of the book.

Our volume is primarily concerned with what is usually called Black Africa – that is the former European colonies lying south of the Sahara – excluding, thereby, the countries of North Africa (from Morocco to Egypt). We also leave aside South Africa, whose history is so distinct as to make comparison difficult at this stage. Furthermore, we are aware that some parts of our analysis do not apply as well to the Horn of Africa, where areas like Ethiopia, Eritrea, Somalia and Northern Sudan have dissimilar social structures and have had a different political experience. We do not, therefore, intend the generic term 'Africans' to be understood as a blanket statement about all the inhabitants of the African continent. Our use of the term 'continent' thus refers to the area defined above.

Finally, we have aimed to present our argument in a concise, compact and reader-friendly book. For this reason, we decided at the outset to impose a strict limit to the size of the volume. Because we wanted the individual chapters to be both accessible separately and easily read, we agreed that they should all have a similar length and that we would keep to the absolute minimum the number of footnotes. This is a book about ideas, arguments and interpretation, not a reference volume. Readers will find in the bibliography only a selection of those works which most usefully stimulated our reflection on African politics.

I

The Informalization of Politics

The first part of the book focuses clearly on the central question of political analysis, that is, how African polities function. Here, we propose the notion of the 'informalization' of politics – in a clear reference to the vast literature on the informal economy – because the parallel seems to us both apposite and enlightening. Not only does it suggest that the 'real' business of politics is taking place where analysts are often not looking, but what is actually happening in the political realm in Africa is more often than not of an 'informal', or personalized, nature.

Although the whole of the book is an attempt to make sense of contemporary African politics, this first part examines explicitly and in detail three key areas of classical political analysis, in Africa (as elsewhere): the place of the state, civil society and the question of elites and leadership. Our approach to these well-worn issues will reveal substantive differences with most current interpretations.

Our argument centres on the analysis of the ways in which the political system, as inherited at independence, has been re-shaped (Africanized as it were) both by the circumstances of the post-colonial period and by the political culture of independent African countries. The rise and fall of the post-colonial patrimonial system has contributed to the sedimentation of a political (dis)order, of which the dominant characteristic is that it is informal and personalized. To understand what is happening in Africa today thus requires that we recast the standard questions of political science in the light of what we might define as the infra-institutional aspects of power.

The first chapter will show how the state in Africa is not just weak but essentially vacuous. The state is self-evidently weak in terms of the Weberian ideal-type: there are on the continent virtually no states able to meet the criteria of the Western, or for that matter of the developing Asian 'tiger', model. It is vacuous because the exercise of central political power has not been emancipated from the overriding dominance of localized and personalized political contests. The state in sub-Saharan Africa has not been institutionalized – in that it has not become structurally differentiated from society – so that its formal structure ill-manages to conceal the patrimonial and particularistic nature of power. This is so partly for good historical reasons – the bureaucratization of the colonized state had been institutionally feeble – and partly for cultural reasons – the personalized nature of prestige and status in African societies. But what we want to stress here, in contrast to most current interpretations, is that there are powerfully instrumental reasons for the informalization of politics.

The second chapter will stress the extent to which the notion of civil society has been abused by those who would see in Africa social movements willing and able to challenge central power. The argument that there are well-conceived and properly organized political forces confronting the 'state' cannot seriously be sustained by the evidence. The reality is that in Africa the substance of politics is to be found in the myriad networks which link the various levels of power, from top to bottom. Here we want to investigate the question of whether such an informal relationship is not best explained by the instrumental quality of the relations between the holders of state power and their various clients throughout society.

The third chapter examines the (political, social and economic) behaviour of African elites. Beyond the many changes in ideology exhibited by political leaders – of which democratization is perhaps the latest – what is most noticeable is the unchanging nature of their ties with society. Representation in Africa appears instrumentally to be connected with a complex nexus of transactional links between the leader, or patron, and his/her clientelistic constituency (both local and national). To focus on political elites is thus to highlight the ways in which power is personalized and how legitimacy continues primarily to rest on practices of redistribution. This too should induce a more careful reconsideration of present 'democratic' political transitions.

1
W(h)ither the State?

The copious literature on the state in sub-Saharan Africa is very largely a dialogue of the deaf. Some argue that such political institutions have pre-colonial roots in the continent. Others contend either that they have not been successfully transplanted from their Western origins or that only now are they in the process of being constructed. While many stress the weakness, if not the evanescence, of the state in contemporary Africa, an almost equal number emphasizes its over-developed and totalitarian nature. Thus, it often seems that analysts are more concerned to find confirmation of their own theoretical or conceptual predilection than to seek to understand the realities of the structure of political power as they are in fact to be found in post-colonial African societies.

It is true that the analysis of the configuration of present political institutions is not easy. There have always been contested political interpretations of the genesis, development and functioning of the modern state. Equally, there has seldom been agreement on the causal significance of state formation for the development of modern society, in the West or elsewhere. Nevertheless, it is quite clear that there are a number of paradigms on the institutionalization of power which simply fail convincingly to account for the role of the state in contemporary Africa.

Our intention here is less to review the relevance of present debates than to assess the extent to which existing conceptualizations contribute to an understanding of the exercise of power as it can be observed empirically on the continent. Our starting point lies with the Weberian approach to the formation of the modern state: less, it must be said, in terms of the celebrated notion of the monopoly of legitimate violence than from the thesis which its author develops on why the overcoming of patrimonialism is a prerequisite to the successful emergence of the state.

Our own argument is that the state in Africa was never properly institutionalized because it was never significantly emancipated from society. That it was not, has to do partly with historical factors linked to the specific development of the colonial state – a state both arbitrary and poorly bureaucratized – and partly with important cultural considerations, which we shall discuss in greater detail in Part II of this book. Above all, however, it is the consequence of the fundamentally instrumental concept of power which marks out what we call the informalization of politics on the continent. There are, in consequence, good grounds for thinking that the weak character of the state in Africa may be more perennial than has hitherto been envisaged. It may well be, therefore, that the state in contemporary Africa will durably fail to conform to our own Western notions of political modernity.

The non-emancipated state

Existing debates on the complexion of the African state may well appear academic. This is because they often reflect *a priori* disagreements on definition between analysts belonging to different scholarly or theoretical traditions. A well-considered reflection on the subject, however, is of considerable practical importance for the analysis of contemporary African politics. Such debates have a direct bearing on what we think is currently happening on the continent. In this chapter, we shall not attempt to give an exhaustive account of the conceptual disagreements[1] dividing analysts. We shall in the first instance focus on what we believe to be three of the most prevalent interpretations of the state in order to show how they tend either to remain excessively teleological or to neglect relevant cultural considerations.

The first approach, common to a number of anthropologists and historians, assumes that any relatively centralized political structure presiding over the destiny of the peoples of a given geographical area can be assimilated to a state. If such are indeed some of the necessary attributes of the modern state, they are not in and of themselves sufficient to its formation, and even less its consolidation. The state is not merely the 'inevitable' result of the evolution of a system for the regulation of power within the social order. The development of a modern state

---

[1] For a review of the literature on the state and for an examination of the colonial state, see Chabal, 1992, Chapter 4.

depends above all on the gradual emancipation of established political structures from society.

The second, favoured by those who write within a Marxist or neo-Marxist perspective, is that the state is simply the instrument of accumulation and violence wielded by a dominant social class – in their parlance, the superstructure. Such an approach is misleading. On the one hand, it is difficult to establish, other than in ideological terms, whether there are in Africa identifiable social classes with discrete and coherent political ambitions. On the other, it is self-evidently the case that the modern state (whether in the West or in Asia) has been instrumental in fostering and co-ordinating economic growth for the benefit of a large array of social classes – and not just of the political elites. In any event, it is not even clear that such elites do make up a class, even in Marxian terms.

The third, on the origins of African polities, tends to confuse appearance with reality. The fact that all post-colonial states have been formally constituted on the model of the modern Western state is not in itself evidence of the degree of their institutionalization. Above and beyond the public display of the attributes of the modern state – such as ministries or the civil service – the reality of the exercise of power on the continent points to a necessary caution when it comes to assessing the degree to which such formal bodies do amount to a modern (Weberian) state. Is the official proclamation of the rule of law, for instance, not often deceptive?

For our part, we approach the question from the perspective of the Weberian tradition. We would thus argue that a proper understanding of the informalization of politics must be grounded in a more resolutely sociological approach. From this viewpoint, the modern state is the outcome of a process by which the realm of politics is gradually emancipated from society and constituted into increasingly autonomous political institutions. The key to such institutionalization is not so much the gradual acquisition of the monopoly of legitimate violence (though that, as Weber rightly emphasized, is obviously important) as the successful establishment of a truly independent bureaucracy. The emancipation of the state thus rests on the establishment and operation of a civil service unconstrained by the dynamics of social pressures.

The implication of such an analysis is that the emergence of the modern state means the end of patrimonialism – that is, following Weber, a complete break from the notion that the holders of political power possess any legitimate claim on the assets or resources which they administer. The public and private spheres become functionally distinct. By contrast, the patrimonial model implies an instrumentally profitable lack of distinction between the civic and personal spheres.

The ruler allocates political office to his clients on the basis of patronage, rather than according to the criteria of professionalism and competence which characterize the civil service.

Such a modern bureaucracy, however, is only possible in a context where, *inter alia*, appointment and advancement are based on meritocracy, where salaries are commensurate with responsibility and are paid on time, and where there is a real (as opposed to imaginary) bureaucratic career structure. It is at this price that the state functionaries cease to be 'patrimonial servants' and begin to conceive of the legally and professionally distinctiveness of their role.[2] On these grounds alone, it would be fair to say that there is today no such civil service on the continent. The state in Africa is thus not institutionalized. Why this should be so, is one of the key questions which this chapter addresses.

Furthermore, as other political sociologists have made clear, the development of the modern state implies the emergence of a notion of citizenship binding individuals directly to the state – above and beyond the more proximate ties of kinship, community or faction. That such is not the reality in post-colonial Black Africa should not surprise us since it is clear that the institutionalized political structure to which Weber alluded is an ideal-type and has, historically, been the exception rather than the rule. Nevertheless, the extent to which the state is endowed with the characteristics outlined above is an important consideration from the analytical standpoint. It is true that such a perspective on the 'modernity' of the African state and the nature of power in Africa can sometimes be construed as Eurocentric.[3] Yet it remains one of the very few approaches enabling us to assess comparatively the relationship between state and society in the modern world.

To show that the contemporary African 'state' operates according to criteria far removed from those presented above is not difficult. We could look, for example, at the reality of recruitment to state-salaried employment on the continent. It is common knowledge that appointments to positions of 'public' responsibility, even at a fairly junior level, are very largely made according to the wishes of the political leaders. The overriding criterion for selection is (kin, communal or other types of) loyalty to the ruling elites rather than qualification or competence. The head of the national radio of a major West African country confided recently that he was constantly under pressure to hire relatives of

---

[2] See here Part III, Chapter 6, in H. Gerth and C. Wright Mills (eds), *From Max Weber: Essays in Sociology* (London: Routledge, 1991).

[3] See, as one example of African sensitivity, the conclusions of a volume on the French Revolution edited in Nigeria: Emeka Nwokedi and Jean-Pascal Daloz (eds), *French Revolution: a Nigerian perspective* (Ibadan: Macmillan, 1990).

the members of the political elites. He explained that to resist such pressure would inevitably mean he would lose his job. According to him, it had thus become virtually impossible to employ properly qualified and experienced radio personnel.[4]

Even ignoring the most blatant cases of nepotism – such as, for instance, that of Bokassa in the Central African Republic – it is clear that the practice of appointment to state employment on ascriptive or personalized grounds is the norm on the continent. Moreover, it would be naive to think that the political transitions which have taken place since 1990 have brought about any significant changes in this respect. Looking at two countries which are often taken as pioneers of democratization – Benin and Zambia – merely confirms this observation. Benin's elected president, N. Soglo, is commonly acknowledged to have become markedly more nepotistic over time, while his Zambian counterpart, F. Chiluba, sacked the director of national television for stating publicly that too much air-time was devoted to the Born Again movement, to which Chiluba belongs.

An analysis of the norms regulating the civil service would reveal the degree to which the state in Africa is far removed from the ideal-type outlined above. In Nigeria, for example, it often seems that there are as many rules as there are employees. Mind-bending punctiliousness lives side by side with the most relaxed approach to regulations so that in practice there are within the same service instances of obstinate bureaucratic obstruction and well-practised accommodation. Thus, holders of state office, however lowly, are rarely 'impartial'. Either they pursue their own 'business' interests – that is the negotiation of their service for a fee – or else they provide the favour which is expected, sometimes demanded, for clearly understood patrimonial reasons.

In short, therefore, the logic of state service is resolutely particularistic and personalized – far removed from the bureaucratic norms as they operate willy-nilly in most Western societies. Is this because the Western bureaucratic model has not been properly assimilated or because that model makes no sense in the real world in which most Africans live? There appears in this respect to be a sense of resigned fatalism: it is expected that civil servants will abuse their power. Whatever the reasons for such attitudes, many of which will be explored in the course of this book,[5] the clear and unambiguous outcome is that public employment is exploited as a private resource. State bureaucratic institutions are thus rarely more than empty shells.

We could provide countless other illustrations of the ways in which the state in Africa is not properly institutionalized. The authors, for

---

[4] Personal (and confidential) communication to one of the authors, June 1997.
[5] Most particularly in Chapter 7 on corruption.

example, know of a particular Congolese ministry bereft of bureaucratic memory since the archives are destroyed with each regime change. Another revealing fact is that there is on the continent no country with a functioning system of personal taxation. More generally, it can be shown that civil servants consider the edicts of their political masters to override any regulation to which those selfsame masters may officially subscribe. In a situation where the most basic rules of bureaucratic accountability are flouted at will, there cannot be in post-colonial Africa the most elementary institutional infrastructure which would make it possible to sustain the modern state, as it is understood in the West.

It is, of course, true that there are significant differences in respect of the norms of bureaucratic efficiency between African countries. Somalia, Liberia, the two Congos and Chad are at one end of the spectrum, Zimbabwe at the other – leaving aside the admittedly very different case of South Africa. It serves no purpose to generalize excessively and to reduce all African political systems to their lowest common denominator. At the same time, however, let us avoid the opposite excess, which consists in arguing that no generalization is possible because there are in Africa fifty irredeemably different countries. Beyond the existing diversity, it is clear that any serious study of the state in Africa brings to light a number of analytically significant similarities.[6] Most particularly, it reveals that forty years after the first independences, Africa remains bereft of the degree of political institutionalization necessary to the emergence of the modern state, as defined above. On the contrary, the empirical evidence seems to suggest that the political realm is becoming ever more informalized.

Instrumentalization and the undifferentiated state

There is little consensus on the nature of the state in Africa, even on the fact that it is both poorly emancipated and very largely patrimonial. If in some cases it is merely a mirage, in most others it is in productive symbiosis with society (as we explain in the next chapter). For us it is, in Weberian terms, no more than an artificially 'modern' political edifice. Although such a conclusion would be strenuously denied by the African political elites, for whom the state is (among others) a token of international respectability, it is of the greatest significance for political analysis.

[6] On this very point, see Médard, 1991.

In the remainder of this chapter, we shall examine the three most common analytical interpretations of the post-colonial state on the continent. The first is the neo-patrimonial model derived directly from Weberian sociology. The other two – the hybrid state perspective and the paradigm of the transplanted state – both issue from a biological analogy. We shall then outline our own approach.

The neo-patrimonial approach seeks to make sense of the (real or imaginary) contradictions to be found in the state in sub-Saharan Africa.[7] From this perspective, the state is simultaneously illusory and substantial. It is illusory because its *modus operandi* is essentially informal, the rule of law is feebly enforced and the ability to implement public policy remains most limited. It is substantial because its control is the ultimate prize for all political elites: indeed, it is the chief instrument of patrimonialism. The state is thus both strong and powerless, overdeveloped in size and underdeveloped in functional terms. Although there are important differences among Black African countries in this respect, what it is significant to emphasize is that, from this perspective, the character of the state is determined by the degree to which the existing political order is institutionalized.

The merit of the neo-patrimonial model is twofold. First, it makes it possible to account for the undeniable fact that the public and the private spheres largely overlap. Second, it helps to explain in which ways the operation of a political system is no longer entirely 'traditional' – hence the weight of the prefix *neo*. In the post-colonial context, political legitimacy derives from a creatively imprecise interaction between what might be termed 'ancestral' norms and the logic of the 'modern' state. The edifice conforms to the Western template while the workings derive from patrimonial dynamics. Within a neo-patrimonial system the much trumpeted 'public' sector is in reality appropriated by private interests. The consequence is double: on the one hand, public service remains personalized by way of clientelism and nepotism; on the other, access to the public institutions of the state is seen as the main means of personal enrichment – even if the fruits of such labour are thereafter to be redistributed or even reinvested.

For its part, the hybrid state perspective focuses on the effects for politics of the mixing of the Western norms introduced under colonial rule and the values inherent to African social systems.[8] While the neo-patrimonial approach emphasizes the failure of political institutional-

[7] The main proponent of this approach is Jean-François Médard who, following in the footsteps of such pioneering studies as Eisenstadt, 1972, has applied these concepts to Black Africa. See Médard, 1982 and 1991.

[8] See here chiefly Jean-François Bayart, *L'Etat en Afrique: la politique du ventre* (Paris: Fayard, 1989) and 'L'historicité de l'Etat importé' in Jean-François Bayart (ed.), *La greffe de l'Etat* (Paris: Karthala, 1996).

ization on the continent, that of the hybrid state stresses the success of the rise of a genuinely different 'indigenous' African state. In other words, this second paradigm offers an argument about the reappropriation and *successful* adaptation of the Western model of the state to the African context. According to this view, the African state, erected upon the artificial national boundaries drawn by the colonial powers, has been reshaped according to local political practices. Furthermore, the state has been utilized as the instrument of 'primitive accumulation' achieved through the monopoly seizure of the means of production by the political elites.

This approach concentrates on the analysis of the specific history of the colonial and post-colonial trajectory of the diverse types of states to be found in Africa today. It makes clear how the quest for state hegemony on the continent may have distinct outcomes according to existing differences in the political configuration of power struggles and in the social inequalities extant. This approach develops a theory of the 'rhizome state' in which the visible institutional branches are less significant than the subterranean roots issued from the complex world of factional struggles and local rivalries. It makes it possible conceptually to analyse the 'African' state, despite the singularities of its own deep history, in ways which enable comparisons with the Western state.

The paradigm of the rejection of the transplanted state, on the other hand, turns on the notion that the wholesale transfer of the Western state to Africa has *failed* very largely because of cultural factors.[9] The model of the modern Western European state, itself the outcome of a most singular historical development, cannot simply be transported to a wholly different socio-cultural setting. Though both the institutions and the trappings of the Western state have now become ubiquitous, they acquire entirely different meanings and operate radically differently outside their original habitat. The result is that the political system thus established, while formally reminiscent of its origins, is re-shaped by local conditions to such a degree that it comes to be used for thoroughly different purposes. Often, large elements of the original model are discarded or cease to function altogether. The transplanted state, therefore, is no longer the modern Western state nor is it properly a hybrid. It is generically distinct.

[9] Culture is here understood (following both Weber and Geertz) not merely as shared acquired values, norms and beliefs but as that which enables individuals to be mutually intelligible. It is thus possible to belong to a same culture but to have radically different values. The main proponent of this paradigm is Bertrand Badie; see here Badie & Birnbaum, 1979 and Badie, 1992.

This approach is part of a wider current of thought which goes against the once fashionable universalization of paradigms (like development or dependence). Drawing on political sociology, the concept of the state which it elaborates is bound up with the socio-cultural context from which its political structures are drawn. Taken to its extreme conclusion this paradigm would advocate a deterministic notion of politics and a simplified vision of the self-contained autonomy of separate cultural traditions. As it is applied to Africa, however, this approach offers a more temperate argument about the culturally-induced mutations of imported political structures. The contention is that such transformations are so significant that the state to be found today in Africa bears little relation to the original model: it is a ponderously inefficient Leviathan unable even to domesticate internal violence.

Nevertheless, the merit of the three approaches discussed above is that they take seriously the political dynamics of African societies. In this way they undoubtedly constitute an analytical advance on the universalizing *'prêt-à-penser'* fashionable in the 1960s and 1970s. Present-day conceptualization is now much more firmly combined with serious empirical research and well-grounded historical insights. Our concern with all three approaches, however, and more particularly the neo-patrimonial model and the paradigm of the hybrid state, is that they have tended to overestimate the impact of colonialism on the formation of the contemporary African state. Yet it is far from certain that the colonial administrative experience did in fact eradicate 'pre-colonial' political traditions and lay secure foundations for the proper institutionalization of the state after independence.

Colonial rule was neither the fundamental rupture which many envisaged it to be nor a mere interlude in the placid history of the continent. Viewed historically, what it seems most important to emphasize is the significance of the continuities in political practice from the pre- to the post-colonial period.[10] From this perspective, then, it is clear that the type of state established in Africa turned out to be but a mere shadow of the original. That is why the analysis of the political sedimentation of existing political systems must weigh carefully the relevance of the original imported model of the state when it comes to understanding the actual political dynamics of contemporary Africa.

It is in this respect interesting to note that the recent historiography of Africa has led to a more realistic reassessment of the magnitude of the changes which the colonial period induced. Without doubt, the imperial rulers did divide the continent into artificially created terri-

---

[10] For an elaboration of this argument see Chabal, 1992. The question of the importance of culture for development is indeed complex, as we shall show in Chapters 9 and 10.

torial entities with little concern for existing divisions. They certainly did disturb, or even destroy, the existing socio-political communities. The colonial period was unquestionably a time of great change. Nevertheless, the extent of the transformation is often misconstrued. Indeed, since the bureaucratic and political structures put in place were primarily designed to maintain order at the lowest possible cost and to ensure the profitable exploitation of the colonies, they were from the beginning distinct from their metropolitan models.[11]

It is now clear, for example, that at the local level, French district officers (or other assorted *rois de la brousse*) paid little heed to procedure and administered their areas of responsibility with a large degree of discretion. Isolated in the countryside and with ineffectual administrative support, theirs was a lonely task. Unsurprisingly, they tended to discharge their duties in a personalized, arbitrary and 'unofficial' manner which ill contributed to the development of modern bureaucratic order. The British practice of indirect rule, for its part, consisted in administering the colonial territory through established traditional authorities and by means of existing political institutions. Here too, therefore, it is questionable whether colonial administration did much to lay the foundations for a properly emancipated state. As for the Portuguese *chefe de posto*, he was often charged with having gone native altogether, so close was his proximity to the Africans with whom he lived.

The historiography of the colonial period in Africa thus paints a picture of a colonial civil service which sought to devise pragmatic ways of adapting the imperial directives to the administration of its subjects rather than a method of inculcating new political and governmental habits. The need to keep expenditures under control and the search for legitimacy led inevitably to a rather informal management of the colonial territories.[12] For example, justice was more frequently rendered by the colonial administrator than by a magistrate sitting in a court of law. As a result, the ideal-type of the (Weberian) bureaucratic state essentially remained a myth of the colonial mission and there was never much chance that it would survive at independence. Moreover, the colonial experience showed how a 'modern' bureaucracy could be both arbitrary and personalized – characteristics which were infinitely more compatible with existing African practices than the original Western model.

For this reason, the neo-patrimonial model is useful only if it is made clear that colonial bureaucratic institutionalization never man-

---

[11] Though it is probably the case that the more consequential changes had more to do with the collapse of traditional systems of exchange, the introduction of a market economy or missionary proselytizing.

[12] For a recent and very useful synthesis on this question, see Bourmaud, 1997.

aged to overcome the strongly instrumental and personalized characteristics of 'traditional' African administration. Similarly, the paradigm of the hybrid state cannot be taken at face value since the very colonial state which was re-appropriated and re-shaped after independence hardly qualified as a modern Western institution in the first place. The colonial state was but superficially akin to its Western model. Only an approach which concentrates solely on the state as instrument of domination could lose sight of the fact that the African post-colonial state was never functionally differentiated from society. In other words, it is not because state power makes it possible to rule over a given 'national' territory that the state can be said to be meaningfully institutionalized.

Centralization of power is a necessary but not a sufficient condition for the development of a modern (Weberian) state – the fundamental attribute of which is its institutional emancipation from society. Because the African post-colonial state has failed to become differentiated from the society over which it rules, it cannot acquire the neutral political status which alone would allow its legitimation and its proper institutionalization. Such a process would require at the very least that the political system overcome the particularistic constraints which presently govern its very functioning. The realities of contemporary Africa, however, suggest not just that there is no trend in that direction but that, on the contrary (and as we shall see in Part II) there may well be on the continent what we have called a 're-traditionalization' of society.

It is perhaps true that the model of the rejection of the transplanted state, on grounds of cultural incompatibilities, comes closest to an accurate analysis of the political evolution of post-colonial Africa. Nevertheless, what must be made clear is how, in reality, so very little effort was made properly to ensure the successful graft of the Western model. This was due to at least two reasons. First, the hurried manner in which decolonization took place[13] did not augur well for the rooting of the Western model into the local habitat. Second, the readiness of the former colonial powers to overlook the very obvious ways in which the political structures put in place were 'Africanized' after independence testifies to a serious lack of concern about state institutionalization.

Our own approach to the question of the state is different. We start from the empirical realities of contemporary Africa as we can observe them. The paradigm we propose is that of the political instrumentalization of disorder – by which we mean the profit to be found in the weak institutionalization of political practices.

---

[13] Except in the Portuguese territories.

One of our central arguments is that the state is both *vacuous* and *ineffectual*. It is *vacuous* in that it did not consolidate, as was once expected, on the foundations of the colonial legacy but instead rapidly disintegrated and fell prey to particularistic and factional struggles. It became an empty shell. As a result it failed to acquire either the legitimacy or the professional competence which are the hallmarks of the modern state. It is *ineffectual* in that it has never been in the interest of African political elites to work for the proper institutionalization of the state apparatus. Or to put it another way, its usefulness is greatest when it is least institutionalized.

The failure of the state to be emancipated from society has profoundly limited the scope for 'good government' in sub-Saharan Africa. Equally, such a poorly institutionalized state has not had the means seriously to spur sustainable economic growth on the continent. Nevertheless, the very weakness and inefficiency of the state has been profitable to the African political elites. The development of political machines and the consolidation of clientelistic networks within the formal political apparatus has been immensely advantageous. It has allowed them to respond to the demands for protection, assistance and aid made by the members of their constituency communities in exchange for the recognition of the political prominence and social status which, as patrons, they crave. The instrumentalization of the prevailing political (dis)order is thus a disincentive to the establishment of a more properly institutionalized state on the Weberian model. Why should the African political elites dismantle a political system which serves them so well?

Our approach suggests that it is inappropriate to consider the evolution of the African state from the teleological perspective of its putative development along supposedly universal Western lines. The assumption hitherto has been that the state would 'eventually' conform to such universalizing tendencies. Indeed, analysts of contemporary Africa have for too long been enthralled by the notion of political 'development'. It was presumed either that the African elites were in fact working towards the emancipation of the state from society or that the very dynamics of the post-colonial political evolution of African countries would in due course bring about such a modernization of the state. Yet the most cursory examination of the history of the modern Western state would have shown that it did not develop because it was 'programmed' to do so. It was constituted over time in the form we know today because of a very specific, and probably unique, configuration of economic and socio-political dynamics.

For this reason, therefore, we should be prepared to consider whether the informalization of politics in Africa is not likely to prove a defining feature of its socio-political order for the foreseeable future. Will there not in fact continue to be an inbuilt bias against the institutionalization of the state as we know it from the Western experience? Indeed, the current patrimonial and prebendal practices of political elites are (as we shall show throughout the book) most satisfactory, at least from the micro-sociological perspective of the individuals and communities they serve. In such circumstances, then, where would the momentum to abolish or reform them come from? It is most unlikely to arise from civil society, as we shall explain in the next chapter.

Hence, the notion that politicians, bureaucrats or military chiefs should be the servants of the state simply does not make sense. Their political obligations are, first and foremost, to their kith and kin, their clients, their communities, their regions, or even to their religion. All such patrons seek ideally to constitute themselves as 'Big Men', controlling as many networks as they can. But to succeed as a 'Big Man' demands resources; and the more extensive the network, the greater the need for the means of distribution. The legitimacy of the African political elites, such as it is, derives from their ability to nourish the clientele on which their power rests. It is therefore imperative for them to exploit governmental resources for patrimonial purposes.

There is thus a critical contradiction at the heart of the present political condition of sub-Saharan Africa. Proper institutionalization of the state would obviate the need continuously to have to display the substance of one's power. If political domination became embodied in the recognized juridical universe of the bureaucratic state, political elites would no longer have to justify their prominence through the fulfilment of their patrimonial duties.[14] What this would mean, however, is that they would have to accept both the supremacy of institutions over individuals and the temporary nature of their political eminence. Such is the price of institutionalized legitimacy.

Within the ambit of the modern (Weberian) state, office holders lose all right to the ownership of public goods, of which they are but the temporary custodians. In such a political system there can be no patrimonial legitimacy. There are thus strict and legally enforceable limits to the private use of state resources. Such deontology of public service would make it impossible to satisfy the clientelistic demands which are made in Africa. Given the present social and cultural expectations on the continent, what grounds are there for thinking that such demands will cease in the future? What grounds indeed are there for thinking that the present domestic dynamics at work favour the legal bureaucratization of the political order? These are undoubtedly the questions at the heart of any serious analysis of contemporary politics in Black Africa.

---

[14] See Bourdieu, 1980.

We are thus led to conclude that, in most African countries, the state is no more than a décor, a pseudo-Western façade masking the realities of deeply personalized political relations. There may well appear to be a relative institutionalization of the main state structures but such bodies are largely devoid of authority. In Western Europe the Hobbesian notion of the state led to the progressive development of relatively autonomous centres of power, invested with sole political legitimacy. In Black Africa, however, such legitimacy is firmly embedded in the patrimonial practices of patrons and their networks.

At one extreme of the spectrum there are countries, like Somalia, where the very shell of the state has shattered utterly and where politics has become a naked power struggle between warlords.[15] At the other extreme, we find former white settler colonies where, as a result of the attempts made to establish a workable institutional political framework, the state has been more substantially consolidated. Nevertheless, it is significant that in a country like Zimbabwe, the post-colonial Africanization of the political system has brought a relatively rapid erosion of established bureaucratic norms. A large number of the new political elites, anxious to make good the disadvantages they suffered under the Smith regime, are today active participants in the informalization of politics.

More generally, the severity of the current economic crisis in Africa is unlikely to favour the institutionalization of the state. Political elites, bereft of the means of their patrimonial legitimacy, are engaged in an ever more frantic search for the resources which the informalization of politics might generate. Such heightened competition is apt to bring about greater disorder, if not violence. Conversely, there is every chance that the elites will use the reforms currently ushered in by the so-called transitions to democracy in order to secure both renewed legitimacy and access to the new assets which the apparent liberalization of the continent's economies makes available – among others, and somewhat paradoxically, by way of structural adjustment, as we show in Chapter 8.

[15] We discuss the role of political violence in Chapter 6.

2
The Illusions
of Civil Society

Whatever the approach taken to the African post-colonial state, it is clear that the expectations generated by independence have been confounded. There is today a general consensus that the state has patently failed either to contribute to the institutionalization of politics or to spur economic development on the continent. Current thinking stresses the need to cut back or bypass the state, seen as both supremely inefficient and fundamentally predatory, in order to stimulate the more dynamic forces of African societies.

It is within this context that we must examine the increasingly vocal arguments presented by a number of Africanists in favour of the putative role of civil society for the reform of the political realm. Although until the nineteenth century the notion of civil society was virtually synonymous with that of the state, it is commonly taken today to refer to the opposite – namely, that which is outside the state. Vague and idealized as this view may be, it is at present invested with the greatest significance. We shall show in this chapter how difficult it is in practice to use this concept in relation to sub-Saharan Africa.

Our argument is that the dichotomy between state and civil society, which is substantially taken for granted in most current interpretations of African politics, does not reflect realities on the continent. The notion of civil society would only apply if it could be shown that there were meaningful institutional separations between a well organized civil society and a relatively autonomous bureaucratic state. Instead, what we observe in Black Africa is the constant interpenetration, or straddling, of the one by the other. Those who emphasize the role of civil society are thus forced to identify it very largely as a residual category, including as it were all the individuals and groups who express dissent.

The danger of emphasizing this supposed opposition between state and civil society is that it creates the illusion that African political systems are more similar to their Western counterparts than they really are. Yet there is on the continent no genuine disconnection between a structurally differentiated state and a civil society composed of properly organized and politically distinct interest groups. The current assumption about the emergence of such a recognizable civil society in Africa is thus eminently misleading and derives more from wishful thinking or ideological bias than from a careful analysis of present conditions.

A misleading dichotomy

Africanists who use the notion of civil society usually feel the need to explain its limits in the current political situation of the continent, even if they do not always recognize its historical and theoretical origins. Indeed, it is striking how few of them have a properly historical sense of the evolution of the notion in the Western context. We do not intend here to review the literature on civil society, nor indeed to trace its conceptual genesis. We merely want to highlight some of the aspects which we think have had an important influence on the analysis of politics in contemporary Africa.

It is useful to remind ourselves that political theorists have provided wide-ranging, and at times contradictory, definitions of the concept of civil society. Originally a philosophical notion, the idea of civil society was subsequently used, and abused, for political and ideological purposes.[1] The concept, therefore, has been applied politically in different ways. Civil society has, at various times, been seen as a bulwark against anarchy, the Church, the Leviathan state, and most recently against totalitarianism. Hence, the idea of civil society as a counter-hegemonic force has evolved according to the context within which it has been employed.[2] For this reason, there is no accepted genealogy of the concept which would provide an analytically useful framework for the study of African polities. As is often the case with notions which become widely practised and analytically fashionable, it becomes difficult to know whether their heuristic value matches their common currency.

---

[1] It is important to remember here that it is Hegel who first distinguished civil society from the state – the latter being conceived as the regulating institution which made possible the separate operation of the former. Marx, for his part, criticized this view on the ground that the state was the instrument of the domination of civil society.

[2] See Ernest Gellner, 'Civil Society in Historical Context', *International Social Science Journal*, 8 (1991).

Moving now to contemporary Africa, there is some doubt as to how useful the concept of civil society is for the understanding of the continent's politics. Although it is sometimes difficult to make sense of the ways in which the notion has been utilized, the most common view is that civil society refers to those intermediary associations which are capable both of representing the country's various groups and of countering the state's hegemonic ambitions. As a result, it is commonly assumed that the political reform of the continent may depend on the extent to which civil society is able to counteract the stultifying weight of the oppressive state. It is often argued that the most vibrant and innovative sections of society are those linked with Non-Governmental Organizations (or NGOs), associations of active citizens speaking for ordinary people and small-scale but dynamic business groups.

Such assumptions raise awkward questions. First, and most importantly, what is the distinction between society and civil society? Given that the expression 'civil' is now often employed routinely, almost as a reflex, without thinking of its precise meaning, it is difficult to know precisely what the qualifier 'civil' adds to our understanding.[3] Does it connote a certain idea of 'civility', an identifiable arrangement of social activities that makes for a more ordered society? If that is the case, might it not imply a given type of societal evolution, which would come dangerously close to an argument about the comparative merits of more 'advanced' societies where there is indeed a 'civic' civil society?

A more fruitful approach consists in focusing on the capacity of social groups to come together in order to organize politically, above and beyond existing sociological, religious or other cleavages. Here, civil society would amount to the creation of social networks distinct from the state and capable of transcending primordial family, kin or even communal ties. Yet it is difficult to see how this approach applies to the continent, given that African societies are self-evidently not mass societies composed of discrete individuals detached from their communal environment. This in turn raises the question of whether it is possible to consider the defence of ethnic or regional interests as the legitimate political action of a country's civil society?

If we accept that the concept of civil society entails the defence of more general, or collective, interests, do we then admit that it includes clientelistic networks, mafia organizations, fundamentalist or other religious sects?[4] Or should we limit its use to the world of officially recognized bodies, such as economic associations, professional trade

---

[3] See Victor Azarya, 'Civil Society and Disengagement in Africa', in John Harbeson, Donald Rothchild and Naomi Chazan (eds), *Civil Society and the State in Africa* (Boulder, CO: Lynne Rienner, 1994), p. 88.

[4] White, 1996.

unions and other corporate groupings wielding considerable influence? Alternatively, should the notion only be employed to refer to 'modern' organizations based on the division of labour or other 'non-traditional' functional cleavages? Should one, finally, restrict the notion of civil society to 'high', or elite, associations such as those of lawyers, journalists, businessmen, academics, or to 'low', popular, groupings like village associations, squatter defence committees, market traders, unemployed, etc.?

Perhaps the most crucial question, however, concerns the nature of the relation of civil society with the state. Some argue that civil society is defined by its close association with – meaning here access to and influence upon – the state. If that is the case, are we justified in excluding from it all those groupings and associations which have no direct political effect? How then do we conceptualize the politics of civil society? Conversely, what are we to make of those independent organizations whose individual members are co-opted into the ruling circles? Does civil society necessarily imply a counter-force to state power or is it legitimate to consider temporary, if extended, alliances between certain component members of the state and individual groupings within civil society?

These numerous interrogations demonstrate how conceptually elusive the notion of civil society is. Of course, a focus on the political significance of the various social movements and associations to be found throughout society is vital, if only because the state lacks functional autonomy. Nevertheless, we ought not to lose sight of the basic fact that African societies are essentially plural, fragmented and, above all, organized along vertical lines. Socio-political cleavages are usually a matter of fractions, or factional divisions, which occur primarily because of competition for scarce resources. In general, then, vertical divisions remain more significant than horizontal functional bonds or ties of solidarity between those who are similarly employed or professionally linked.

That is why the development of properly grounded associations charged with the defence and promotion of a 'common good' within the public sphere (to take two opposing examples, trade unions and chambers of commerce) is so highly problematic in Africa. Indeed, such attempts at occupational or professional unity are more often than not undermined by internal discords linked to questions of identity or community. Although it might be argued that this difficulty is not unique to the continent, it is clearly significantly greater there than elsewhere in the world. The question, however, is whether the primacy of such vertical and personalized ties on the continent is not such as to invalidate the notion of a functionally based civil society – on the Western model.

It is sometimes argued that civil society can provide the impetus for the regeneration of politics in Africa: a means of making a fresh start from the all-pervasive and corrupt influence of the state. To what extent, however, has there ever been a rupture between the politics of state and civil society south of the Sahara? Are the holders of power, the political elites, functionally or even politically detached from society? Is it not the case, as we discuss in the next chapter, that deeply rooted vertical forms of political accountability on the continent ensure strong political links between 'high' and 'low' politics?

The state is in fact so poorly institutionalized, so weakly emancipated from society, that there is very little scope for conceptualizing politics in Africa as a contest between a functionally strong state and a homogeneously coherent civil society. Admittedly, there are on the continent numerous active groupings which contest state policies and, occasionally, organize political opposition (protests, strikes, non-violent or even violent campaigns) within society. Nevertheless, it is clear that the business of politics is more usually conducted along informal vertical channels of relations (patron-client networks, communal organizations, etc.) linking the elites with the rest of the population. Socio-political rivalries in Africa are rarely the result of a clear-cut public and supra-communal contest. Nor is there evidence that the government's economic orientation or the nature of the regime in place makes much difference to relations between state and society.[5] In Nigeria, for example, the transition to a democratic regime under the Second Republic (1979–83) brought little change in this respect.

Our argument is that the emergence of a properly institutionalized civil society, led by politically independent citizens, separate from governmental structures, is only possible where there is a strong and strongly differentiated state. Only then is it meaningful to speak of a 'counter-hegemonic' civil society. Historically, however, the only instances of the development of civil societies of this type have occurred in Europe – where their formation was fortuitous, or rather unplanned and unpredictable. The situation in contemporary Africa is, at this stage, historically so different that it is hard to see how it could evolve in the same direction – at least in the foreseeable future.

If it is generally true that the nature of the relationship between state and society defines the political complexion of any polity, it is in our view wrong to conceptualize what is happening on the continent in terms of a zero-sum game competition between the two. It is less a matter of the 'revenge' of civil society against the state, as some have argued,[6] than of a complementary and often mutually beneficial interaction between the two. Understanding politics in Africa is a matter of identifying the complexities of the 'shadow boxing' that takes place

---

[5] As Tom Callaghy shows in Callaghy, 1994.
[6] See Jean-François Bayart, 'La revanche des sociétés africaines', *Politique Africaine*, 11(1983).

between state and society. But above all, it is a matter of explaining the myriad ways in which political actors, within both 'state' and 'civil society', link up to sustain the vertical, infra-institutional and patrimonial networks which underpin politics on the continent.

Civil society as ideology

There is no denying that the notion of civil society is popular today among both Africanists and Africans. The question we wish to explore here is whether its prevalence is due to the genuine development of new social movements in Africa or whether it is the result of more instrumental political factors. We shall look more closely in this section at the two most common usages of the concept. The first is linked with the recent liberal ideology on the minimal state, as put forward by the Bretton Woods institutions. The second turns on the assumption that civil society in Africa constitutes a counter-force to the hegemonic ambitions of the state.

Western donor countries, following the lead of the World Bank and the IMF, have become increasingly concerned at the inability of governments in Africa to manage the economy and promote growth. They have advocated a diminution of the role of the state, and structural adjustment programmes have accordingly sought to curb the economic reach of the state on the continent. As a result, there has been a new emphasis on the putative significance of civil society, which has led in turn to a shift of resources towards local NGOs – conceived by the West as the 'representative' bodies of that civil society. The consequences of such a change in donor policy have been immense: NGOs have blossomed everywhere on the continent.

The political significance of such a massive proliferation of NGOs in Africa deserves closer attention. Our research suggests that this expansion is less the outcome of the increasing political weight of civil society than the consequence of the very pragmatic realization that resources are now largely channelled through NGOs. It would thus be naive to think that the advent of NGOs necessarily reflects a transition from the ponderous world of state bureaucracy to that of more flexible 'civic' associations operating beyond the clutch of the state. In our view, it is rather the reflection of a successful adaptation to the conditions laid down by foreign donors on the part of local political actors who seek in this way to gain access to new resources.

Indeed, NGOs are often nothing other than the new 'structures' with which Africans can seek to establish an instrumentally profitable position within the existing system of neo-patrimonialism. Now that foreign aid largely transits through NGOs, resources can be obtained by channels other than those emanating from the state. Nevertheless, although the opening up of new conduits for the procurement of outside funding reduces the ability of the state to monopolize access to donor resources, it does not fundamentally alter the prebendal and patrimonial character of politics on the continent.

Above and beyond the new discourse of NGO ideology (defence of the poor, child protection, the safeguarding of women's interests, the preservation of the environment, the promotion of integrated development, etc.), the political economy of foreign aid has not changed significantly. The use of NGO resources can today serve the strategic interests of the classical entrepreneurial Big Man just as well as access to state coffers did in the past.[7] Leaving aside those cases where NGOs are used purely for commercial purposes,[8] it is as well to recognize that there is today an international 'aid market' which Africans know how to play with great skill. Indeed, there is very little doubt that NGOs spend an excessive proportion of their budget on furnishing their members with sophisticated and expensive equipment (from computers to four-wheel-drive vehicles), leaving all too little for the development projects which justify the work of the NGO in the first place.

We are not arguing here that NGOs are failing entirely in the aims they set for themselves. Nor are we implying that NGOs do not employ sincerely dedicated personnel who want to alleviate poverty and suffering. We merely wish to underline that the explosion in the number of NGOs is not a reflection of the flowering of civil society in the sense in which it is usually understood in the West. It is in reality (rather than fiction) evidence of the adaptation by African political actors to the changing complexion of the international aid agenda. While in the past Cold War rivalries could profitably be used to generate foreign funding, it is today the commitment to the NGO emphasis on the 'development' of civil society which is rewarded, providing thereby the means of fuelling the patrimonial system. The sources of finance have changed; the instrumentalization of foreign aid has not.

The current prominence of the world of consultancy is symptomatic of this evolution. Where, before, badly underpaid academics sought to gain access to the resources of the state, they are today in search of a contract with a foreign NGO.[9] It could, of course, be argued that such a shift in funding works to weaken state-controlled networks and to

[7] See here Médard, 1992.

[8] On the model of a Senegalese NGO we know which imports computers tax-free, ostensibly for educational purposes, and resells them at huge commercial profit on the parallel market.

[9] See Jean-Pascal Daloz, 'Towards the Intellectual Marginalization of Africa?' in Chris Alden and Jean-Pascal Daloz (eds), *Paris, Pretoria and the African Continent: the international relations of states and societies in transition* (London: Macmillan, 1996).

strengthen civil society associations. Yet this would be hard to sub-
stantiate since the resources channelled through NGOs are for the
most part used in the same ways and for the same patrimonial or clien-
telist purposes. Furthermore, NGO-linked networks are inevitably
intertwined with those emanating from the state.

It is revealing in this respect to note that even state officials try to
forge new ties with the local level, where they know that NGOs prefer,
and are often mandated, to operate. Indeed, it is a fundamental tenet
of NGO philosophy to bypass central governmental bodies and to col-
laborate directly with those that are well implanted locally. However
admirable the principle of decentralization and local development is
in theory, its implementation depends entirely on the co-operation and
competence of those local actors with whom NGOs must ultimately
work. There is thus inevitably an objective convergence of interests
between the obligation for NGOs to find local collaborators and the
need for local or pseudo-local elites to gain access to outside resources.

Whatever the short-term effects of such a state of affairs, there is
little doubt that the present profusion of uncoordinated NGO involvement in Africa is unlikely to lead to sustained development. Our argument is that the spread of NGO activities, allied to the collapse of state
resources, is much more eminently favourable to the instrumentalization of disorder than it is to the emergence of a Western-style civil
society. Indeed, the current situation is having the perverse effect of
encouraging some African politicians cynically to exploit the image of
Africa as a helpless and miserable continent in order to prompt the
involvement of NGOs, from which funding and assistance are
expected.

Far from strengthening civil society, therefore, the role of NGOs
could well lead to the hijacking of genuinely needed development aid
by the same old and well established political elites. If this were the
case, it would explain why African states, which ostensibly stand to
lose most from the involvement of NGOs at local level, continue to
facilitate their work. Where NGOs have become one of the main
sources of foreign aid, the holders of state power will ensure both that
they gain access to these outside resources and that their countries
continue to 'merit' NGO involvement – even if it means 'marketing' the
suffering of their population.

The second question we wish to investigate is that of the supposed
counter-hegemonic role of civil society. Here civil society is seen as the
repository of political resistance to the centralizing and totalitarian
tendencies of the African (one-party) state. Examples of recent popular protest, linked as they are to the transition to multi-party politics,
are often cited as evidence of the potential force of organized civil
society. We would argue, however, that this interpretation is in large

part derived from an unwarranted transposition of what happened in the formerly communist countries of Eastern Europe. Indeed, in our view, both the nature of civic associations and their role in the democratic transition in the former Soviet Bloc bear very little resemblance to what is currently taking place in post-colonial sub-Saharan Africa.[10]

The view that civil society in Africa could act as an opposition to the state is marred by a confusion between political argument and analysis. It rests on the assumption that the post-colonial state on the continent is actually hegemonic. But is this really the case? Although undoubtedly repressive, and occasionally murderous, the African (single-party) state has lacked the organizational skills and the coercive means of the totalitarianism found in Eastern Europe, the Soviet Empire or the Asian communist regimes. There is, in any event, little evidence that African governments ever possessed the resources to underpin their hegemonic ambitions.

Totalitarianism rests on the capacity of a strong, highly institutionalized state to assert absolute control over society. At the very least, it demands command of an efficient coercive apparatus and mastery of a sophisticated network of communications. This has never obtained in sub-Saharan Africa, where the state's authority has rarely extended to the proper regulation of its armed forces, the police or the security services. For this reason alone, we are dubious of the following view: 'The introduction of modern transport, sophisticated weapons and computer power in sub-Saharan Africa has made possible [...] an extraordinary increase in social control: never have rulers possessed greater means of surveillance, control and persuasion over the ruled.'[11] Is this really true? For example, in a country like Nigeria, usually portrayed as the 'giant' on the continent, most cities are devoid of a working telephone network; letters take weeks to reach their destination (when they do arrive) and police officers are seen hitching lifts on public roads. How could totalitarian coercion be exercised in such conditions?

It could be argued that control over public media has enabled states to control information for their own hegemonic purposes. Even here, such a manipulation of the information media is of little significance, for two main reasons. First, virtually all Africans have access to international radio (BBC, Radio France International, Deutsche Welle, etc.) and not a few can now receive satellite television. Second, informal means of communication (from gossip or rumour to the dissemination of news through non-official organizations like ethnic associations or

---

[10] Nowhere in Africa has there been (nor is it clear that there could have been) an equivalent to the Polish trade union movement led by Solidarity.

[11] Jean-François Bayart, 'L'historicité de l'Etat importé', in Jean-François Bayart (ed.), *La greffe de l'Etat* (Paris: Karthala, 1996), p. 17.

African churches) are undoubtedly more efficient and more strongly influential than the official state-controlled media. Moreover, the resources devoted to the official media are regularly mis-employed, thus further weakening their impact. In Zambia, as one of us has been able to observe, large sums have been spent not on improving media coverage in the country but on air-conditioning the television head-quarters.

In our view, therefore, the argument that the state in Africa has managed to achieve hegemonic domination over society remains unconvincing. However arbitrary, violent or even criminal, state coercion on the continent has rarely been such as to make totalitarianism a realistic political option. We would argue instead that, if anything, the very reverse has occurred: it is the state which has been 'captured' by society. Governments in Africa have never achieved the level of institutionalization required of modern totalitarianism; they have remained unemancipated from society. In such circumstances, how can it be seriously argued – as many analysts have done – that the state might have 'devitalized' civil society? There is in Africa little evidence of the type of meaningfully political cleavage between state and civil society which is implied in the above paradigm. On the contrary, what needs to be stressed are the linkages between 'high' and 'low' politics, between the political elites and their clientelistic networks throughout society.

The notion of the counter-hegemonic civil society rests on its potential both to organize politically and to challenge the regime in place. The question we need to address now is whether opposition groups in Africa have a programme of political reform capable of changing the existing political order or whether they merely want to gain power so as to employ it instrumentally according to the selfsame political logic. It is true that, in much of Africa, there is a political opposition genuinely committed to the kind of political reform that would increase political accountability. It is equally true that, in the face of excessive repression, such an opposition is able at times to mobilize strong protest. By and large, however, the tendency in Africa is for political opponents to challenge their exclusion from the state in the hope that their agitation will earn them co-optation. In practice, then, both the cleavage between state and society and the unity of political opposition are more apparent than real – as has been shown repeatedly by the divisions which arise within the opposition as soon as multi-party politics become possible (or, as in Zambia, after the opposition wins the electoral contest).[12]

A dualist, or Manichean, view of the contest between a hegemonic state and a civil society as a potential mobilizing counter-force gen-

---

[12] For a sceptical view on Cameroonian civil society, see Andréas Mehler, 'Cameroun: une transition qui n'a pas eu lieu', in Daloz and Quantin, 1997.

erally fails to account for the extreme fluidity of social and political divisions in sub-Saharan Africa. The example of Nigeria is instructive for it concerns a country in which the politics of civil society have often been claimed to be significant. Like others on the continent, Nigeria is a nation in which most of its people would claim multiple identities – each one of which is determined according to different criteria. The saliency of any particular aspect of this identity changes according to the particulars of a given situation. For example, when religious violence breaks out, people identify with members of their own faith. Thus, conflicts between 'Christians' and 'Muslims' momentarily override any other attribute, whether ethnic, regional or social. A similar process occurs when ethnic identities come to the fore. The weight of each particular form of collective identification is, therefore, contingent on circumstance.

This is, again, easily demonstrated in the Nigerian case when studying inter-communal ties of solidarity within a given geographical area. Typically, a coalition of smaller communities will unite to demand autonomy from a larger and more dominant group. Having achieved their aim, the broader unity will often disintegrate as each group seeks for itself a greater share of the spoils within the new administrative unit. New cleavages now appear leading to new forms of mobilization. Such political strategies result in a high degree of instability, even if there are limits to the number of possible and plausible permutations, due, in part at least, to the lessons drawn from previous experiences. Political rivalry is always liable to create or revive divisions between groups of people, depending on what is at stake and on the influence exercised by political leaders.

The basic reference unit in Nigeria, as elsewhere in Africa, remains family- and kin-based: it is the fundamental 'circle of trust' within which individuals operate. However, the pressures of modern political competition demand that political leaders surround themselves with an ever larger number of dependants. They need continuously to widen their support base. This leads to clientelistic and factional politics, the foundations of which are inevitably more precarious, the further removed they are from that 'circle of trust'. Political elites seek to establish principles of mutual aid, of patron–client reciprocity, based on the model of kin and family relations. These, however, are less solid, more evanescent and depend almost entirely on the extent to which the clientelistic networks are properly nourished. This model of politics obviously applies to Nigeria's civilian political elites.[13] It is equally true of the military regimes, which have been in power for so long. Hence, each and every ministerial reshuffle leads to political tensions.

---

[13] There were no fewer than 215 candidates for the last presidential primaries.

The history of Nigeria, with its recurring cycles of unity and discord, is exemplary of the dilemmas of modern politics in Africa. It demonstrates clearly how, since independence, political leaders aspiring to national office have found themselves torn between their need to transcend the country's social divisions and their inability to operate politically outside. Any serious analysis of the country demands that we reject a simplistic bi-polar view, opposing a single state to a notional civil society, and take into consideration the complexities of the political interaction between the countless socio-economic subsystems which constitute Nigeria.

The paradigm of 'politics from below' (*le politique par le bas*), evolved in France in the 1980s,[14] was undoubtedly a necessary corrective to the interpretative simplifications of developmentalist and dependency theories, with their excessive institutional focus. It brought a welcome shift of analysis to hitherto neglected political processes within society at large. However, this change of perspective has led to an emphasis on the dichotomies between state and civil society which fails to account for their straddling. As we have stressed throughout this chapter, what matters above all are the vertical and personalized ties which link 'high' and 'low' politics, the legitimacy of which is accepted by all, whether at the top or the bottom.

In the absence of an institutionally autonomous and relatively impartial state affording protection to the country's 'citizens', it is imperative for ordinary people to maintain links with those who have power (albeit limited) by playing on ties of primordial solidarity (nepotism) or of clientelism (since all patrons need followers). That is why the legitimacy of the 'Big Man', which rests on his capacity to redistribute resources to his clients, is only questioned when he fails as a patron – which is the exception rather than the norm.

This is not to deny that African socio-political systems are far from egalitarian, but simply to stress that it is not useful to conceptualize them in terms of straightforward divisions between the rulers and the ruled, the elites and the populace. Most political actors are simultaneously dominant and dominated, one of the links in one of the many chains of dependence. Although there are strong inequalities within clientelistic relations, it is well to remember that patrons suffer considerable constraints. The maintenance of their status is entirely dependent on their ability to meet the expectations of their clients – clients who are, as it were, the material embodiment of their standing – and who in turn must placate their own clients. The acuteness of apparent inequalities is reduced by the imperative to be seen to redistribute on a scale appropriate to one's standing.

---

[14] By some of the founding members of the review *Politique Africaine*.

Whether rooted in primordial or clientelistic ties, social relations are inevitably based on personalized bonds of mutually beneficial reciprocity. The demands of such networks frequently force patrons to act against their own immediate economic self-interests – such as, for example, greater investment in their business – in order to meet the obligations on which their social rank and political authority depend. Their long-term political interests, therefore, are often in conflict with their short- or even medium-term potential as business-men or entrepreneurs. That is why, as we shall discuss in greater detail later, there is often in Africa an inherent contradiction between political pressure on economic elites and the requirements of eco-nomic growth and development.

Although the *politique par le bas* approach has made possible a number of newer and more fruitful interpretations, some of the work derived from it has been excessively simplistic, if not Manichean. At times, the emphasis has been placed on the supposed antagonistic dichotomies between state and civil society, so that 'low' politics has been endowed with unwarranted militant or even subversive poten-tial.[15] The paradigm is only useful if it is made clear that the relations between state and society are complex: 'high' politics is both many-sided and intertwined with 'low' politics. What occurs at the top is often grasped only through an examination of the interconnected political relations between 'high' and 'low', between patrons and their clients, between the rulers and the ruled.[16]

In the previous chapter we explained how state politics was not insti-tutionally differentiated from society. Here it is important to stress that social relations in Africa defy the usual developmental expectation: indeed, there are precious few indications that they are becoming organic, or functionally determined by the changing nature of the 'modern' divi-sion of labour. There are, of course, very compelling cultural reasons for this – which we explore in detail in other chapters – among which reli-gious beliefs and the personalized aspects of African forms of identity are paramount. Such attributes, however, are changing over time under the force of socio-economic development. The question we need to confront here is why, despite such change, there has been so little modification in the nature of the political relations between elites and populace.

We believe the answer to this lies in the instrumental nature of pol-itics in Africa. We have shown in Chapter 1 how, despite the institu-tional façade of the state, it has been profitable (at least until the most recent economic crisis) for a large proportion of the population to continue to operate according to the informal norms of vertical, per-

---

[15] For an assessment of writings on 'political derision', see Daloz, 1996.
[16] For a more in-depth discussion of these considerations, see Chabal, 1992, pp. 96–7.

sonalized and infra-institutional relations between state and society. Similarly, there may now be good politically instrumental reasons why, given the present political and economic conditions attached to foreign aid, it might be convenient today to give the impression that civil society is flourishing on the continent.

That such is in practice not the case is revealed particularly clearly in Africa's cities. According to the tenets of the sociology of development, urbanized individuals become increasingly detached from the 'traditional' personalized relations characteristic of social life in rural areas. In the cities, high population densities, the mixing of ethnic groups and the intermingling of professions should all favour more individualized social conditioning. Yet what occurs is usually the reverse: urban dwellers appear to replicate the type of informal and personalized social rapport which is the hallmark of 'traditional' African life. City quarters tend to mirror regional or ethnic divisions. Welfare organizations and even traditional banking ('tontines') thrive – in part, of course, because they offer some form of (morally binding) social protection which no state institution could equal.

We need to recognize that, far from modernizing in the sense in which development theory had anticipated, the continent appears to be moving in the direction of greater informalization. Africa is not institutionalizing, nor is it becoming a mass society. There are today south of the Sahara virtually no examples of social or political relations devoid of clientelistic calculations or considerations of identity. Which is not to say that such relations are not conducted rationally, but merely to explain how that rationality fits into the greater logic of the realm of factional or community imperatives. It is not surprising, therefore, that there is no significant development of horizontal, functionally determined, ties of solidarity – such as professional associations or issue-based groupings.

Our conclusion is twofold. First, Africa is not moving backward; it is not engaged in a notional return to the 'age-old' ways of the continent. Rather, it is pursuing its own specific form of modernization. Second, there is as yet no evidence of functionally operating civil society in Africa. There are, it is true, instances of embryonic societal movements opposing central power (though as yet far removed from the ideals of civil society). Because, however, there is little distinction between the private and public domains and because the organizational capacity of such movements is still limited, it would be misleading to argue that there is a politically salient cleavage between 'state' and 'society'. Instead of focusing on such vague categories it is more profitable to pay attention to the actual behaviour of the main political actors.

3

Recycled Elites

The analysis of post-colonial political systems in Africa is all too often conducted at an excessively abstract level. There is frequently a temptation to wallow in tendentious and rather sterile discussions about ill-defined notions instead of studying political realities as they appear to us empirically. We think it important to move away from interpretations based on a rather vaguely defined sociology of macro-entities such as civil society or class. A more concrete approach centred on the actual behaviour of leaders and other political actors in relation to the rest of the population is in our view far more convincing and far more likely to make sense of what is occurring on the continent.

The previous two chapters have shown that power in Africa is very weakly institutionalized and remains essentially personalized and particularistic. For this reason, we believe that students of African politics should pay special attention to the question of elites and the key issue of leadership. Surprisingly, they rarely do. Most work on those who hold a dominant, or commanding, place in society is concerned with normative, rather than analytical, aspects. For example, developmentalists look for evidence of Westernization while dependency theorists readily assume the elite to be a bourgeoisie. A very large number of studies simply focus on the individual characteristics (qualities or defects) of African leaders, as though it was possible to study them divorced from their place in society.

Yet we would argue that explaining the various ways in which elites in power are connected to those from whom they receive support – that is, in effect, making sense of the complexities of political representation – is fundamental to the comparative understanding of contemporary African politics. That is why we explore in this chapter the extent to which the social role of political notables and the prevailing notion of leadership might provide an explanation for the conspicuous absence of elite change on the continent. We are particularly interested here in uncovering the reasons why the recent transitions to multi-party politics have largely failed to sweep away the old political guard.

On the limited renewal of political actors

It is often argued that the present misfortunes of many African countries are primarily the consequence of the incompetence and dishonesty of their leaders: a change at the top would improve matters considerably. In other words, there is a tendency to attribute the failings of the continent to the individual (moral and political) shortcomings of its rulers, without (in our view) paying proper attention to the workings of the political system as a whole. Although such an approach is entirely understandable in a context where power is so strongly personalized and where the cult of the supreme master is common currency, it is in our view inimical to analysis.

Whatever the defects of African leaders, we are compelled to take note of their durability, their ability to wield power, regardless of the political vagaries of regime change or ideological trends. It is true that the authoritarian nature of the African post-colonial order, with its concentration of power at the very top, is not friendly to the renewal of political elites. Because of this situation, it is frequently assumed that Africans would do away with such well-entrenched politicians if they were given the opportunity. But is this really the case? And if it is, why is it that some of the former African 'dictators' – as in Benin or Madagascar – have recently been re-elected in recognizably 'free and fair' multi-party elections? Could it be merely because they have changed their ideological spots?

Classical political analysis (such as Marx's class struggle or Pareto's circulation of elites) has long stressed that societal crises lead to significant changes amongst the ruling elites. Fundamental economic change or political failure is sanctioned by a radical sweep of the power holders. The African experience, however, would point rather to the arguments developed by Schumpeter or Lasswell about the elites' flexibility and their capacity for adaptation. Empirically, even the most cursory examination of post-colonial Africa would confirm that there has been a very limited renewal of the major political actors.[1] Underneath the present froth of multi-party elections, there is surprising permanence at the top.

---

[1] We reject the notion of a ruling 'class', as we explain below, both because the realm of politics is not sufficiently differentiated from society and because there is hardly any evidence of 'class solidarity' among political elites.

A more detailed study of the members of parliament and government and of those moving in ministerial and presidential circles reveals a high degree of continuity in personnel, including in those countries which have undergone regime changes in the recent multiparty transitions. The supposed new leaders are more often than not experienced politicians with a durable career in the higher echelons of government or administration – even if they had long been out of power on the eve of the last elections. Conversely, it is striking to observe how few fresh political figures have emerged in the immediate past other than through military coups.[2]

Although it is true that African youth is strongly instrumental in mobilizing the opposition for political change, and that many young candidates participate actively in electoral campaigns, they are more often than not sidelined after the vote. Furthermore, contrary to the assumptions made in much recent Africanist writing on the present political transitions, there is little evidence that the rise to power of a younger generation of leaders brings about significant reforms in the political order. As time passes, it is becoming increasingly difficult to argue that, where it occurs, the renewal of political leadership brings about greater 'democratization'. Indeed, there are no convincing examples that such might be the case.

Student protest is undoubtedly strong south of the Sahara, as is support for a variety of radical or revolutionary ideas imported into the continent. And it is certainly not to be doubted that a considerable number of disenfranchised young people yearn for less arbitrary politics.[3] Yet Africa is replete with former youth rebels who have been successfully co-opted and enjoy flourishing careers in the mainstream of state employment or private enterprise. Ideological conviction is easily swayed by access to the means of power. Equally, there is a strong feeling among the younger generation that 'it is our turn to "eat" (that is, reap the benefits from the "system")', especially now that the economic crisis has reduced the range of available resources. Furthermore, current nepotistic practices, by which the elites provide employment for their families and other clients, also go against the determination of radical youth to undermine the existing political order.

Cultural explanations of the longevity of political elites, with their emphasis on the importance of experience and respect for the more aged, do probably make some sense of what is happening. Most African societies continue to subscribe to what might be called a system of deference vis-à-vis the elders, and age (or age group) matters

[2] Such coups, which often propel to the top very young military officers, seem indeed to be one of the very few ways in which to ensure a renewal of political generations.
[3] As Paul Richards has discovered in his research on youth in Sierra Leone. See Richards, 1998.

socially and politically. Contrary to the Western view that youth is the most desirable station in life, adolescent Africans hanker after the age which will endow them with an authority currently denied. When they lie about their age it is to make themselves older, not younger. Similarly, youthful leaders aspire to a title or appellation which will confer upon them the legitimacy of authority that comes with age and maturity.

Our view, however, is that it is far more important to stress the instrumental aspect of age, and thereby the question of access to resources. Aspirants to political office require both credibility and the means to fulfil their ambition. They must be rich enough to become convincing. Inevitably, it is the earlier (largely prebendal) accumulation of wealth – as was possible in the heyday of the 1960s and 1970s when state coffers were still swollen – which gives the older generation the edge over younger political actors. Newcomers have little to offer except their aspiration to 'change' the political system. They do not easily appear to be credible patrons, even if their electoral objectives point to a desire to address the most pressing ills of their country. In the end, voters want to know whether the potential leader will be able to call upon significant resources.

This is well illustrated by the case of Zambia – commonly viewed, following the peaceful electoral removal in 1991 of Kenneth Kaunda, as a model of smooth political transition in Africa. Opposition to the regime came from the Movement for Multi-Party Democracy (MMD), which managed successfully to gain wide support from those who were either politically discontented or dissatisfied with the economy, and in particular, food shortages. From the outset, the MMD was a mixed and variegated coalition including landholders and businessmen supporting financial and trade liberalization, intellectuals in favour of radical change, the bulk of the trade union movement, young graduates in search of employment, as well as a large number of former members of the Kaunda regime.

There was thus a clear division between two types of MMD supporters. On the one hand, there were 'Big Men' ready to play the card of renewal, safe in the knowledge that their financial support for the opposition would give them pride of place in the new regime. On the other, there was a variety of younger hopefuls, often politically sophisticated and well informed about the world beyond Africa, but largely bereft of the resources required to acquire sufficient political prominence. Since the first group did not include any obvious candidate for leadership, they readily threw their support behind Frederick Chiluba (the rising star from the second group) with a reputation for having hitherto steadfastly refused co-optation into the ruling circles.

The evolution of Zambian politics in the 1990s can thus largely be explained by the problems intrinsic to this necessary but unstable alliance between a new leader with little room for manoeuvre and a large array of supporters expecting rapid pay-offs. In order to satisfy their demands, the new president rapidly resorted to old-style practices of governance and, despite his pronouncements, effectively renounced any attempt at a radical reform of the political system.[4] In effect, Chiluba was torn between the requirements of international donors, the demands of his powerful backers and the expectations of the population at large.

He thus faced contradictions between his original promise to reform and the distributive imperatives on which his short-term legitimacy rested. The result was that he failed to satisfy any of his disparate constituencies. Outside aid donors deplore the continued presence in government of incompetent or corrupt ministers (some implicated in drug trafficking). Younger MMD members resent the importance in government given to prominent members of the former regime. Middle-ranking leaders, disappointed not to have been rewarded and obsessed by ethnic and regional rivalries, rush to create new opposition parties. Ordinary Zambians realize that the promises made by the new president have failed to materialize and that they still need to rely on patronage. The situation has evolved somewhat recently since Chiluba has become more wealthy (that is, more resourceful) and thus more self-assured. Nevertheless, clientelism still reigns supreme – from the heart of government, where there is infighting between factions, to the most local level of administration.

The Zambian example shows clearly how an empirical approach, paying particular attention to the behaviour of the different political actors, is infinitely richer than any framework which relies on simplistic oppositions. It is, of course, tempting to highlight the political strength of civil society, the success of all-conquering counter-elites, given the crucial role played by Zambian trade unions in the recent 'democratic transition'.[5] Nevertheless, the prominence in Chiluba's regime of 'recycled' elites, as well as the use of well-worn governing practices to ensure a continuous hold on power, does cast doubt on the reformist potential of the new administration. In truth, it is far from clear that the introduction of fresh arrangements for the election of political leaders induces any in-depth change in political culture.

---

[4] In 1993, for example, he sought to resolve a dubious political crisis by resorting to a state of emergency, harking back to a legal weapon used repeatedly by Kaunda since independence. The 1996 constitutional reform, aiming, among others, at preventing Kaunda – who was widely expected to return to power by electoral means – from standing in the presidential elections, is another instance of the dubious 'democratic' character of his regime. For a multi-disciplinary approach to contemporary Zambia, see Daloz and Chileshe, 1996.

[5] As Michael Bratton does in 'Civil Society and Political Transitions in Africa' in John Harbeson, Donald Rothchild and Naomi Chazan, 1994.

The re-election of previously unpopular leaders like Kérékou in Benin (seen as the pioneer country in the recent political transitions in French-speaking Africa) or Ratsiraka in Madagascar is somewhat puzzling. There are two possible, but sharply opposed, interpretations. Either it is a throwback to the old order, symbolized by some of its wiliest practitioners, or it stands as a symbol of the success of new 'democratic' contests in which free elections enable the voters to change their minds at will. Whatever the case, it raises interesting questions about popular expectations, the vagaries of voting and, more generally, about the significance of the present multi-party political experiments on the continent. Avoiding the usual Eurocentric explanations, it is instructive in this respect to examine, empirically, what public opinion makes of the comeback of these former dictators.

In Benin's capital, Cotonou, one often hears that 'whoever has already eaten can return to power', or that the 'chameleon' has changed his spots. Kérékou has regained credibility by admitting his past sins, giving the benign impression of having become an attentive 'clergyman', and by playing the masterful hand of coalition politics against Soglo, the man who had defeated him in the first multi-party elections. The story is similar in Madagascar, where popular wisdom has it that 'a crocodile which has already eaten is no longer dangerous'. In other words, well-endowed politicians are more likely than others to pay attention to the obligations of generosity which they are expected to discharge, and to ensure that those who support them also 'will eat properly'. The notion of political legitimacy is thus based on the expectation of the 'sharing of the spoils' which is at the heart of the paradigm we propose.

If such old-style political leaders manage to regain the centre-stage, it is likewise because they are exceedingly adept at knowing how to change both style and discourse. African politicians today cannot expect to draw support by pointing to their anti-colonial credentials or by exploiting Cold War rivalries. The ideologies of nationalism, development, or 'authenticity' have exhausted their appeal and there is a need for a fresh approach. Legitimation depends now on the adoption of the currently fashionable notions of liberalization, pluralism, democracy, human rights, rule of law, good governance and even structural adjustment. The new international order dictates such ideological conversions for all countries wanting to ensure foreign aid – on which most African regimes are increasingly dependent.[6]

Nevertheless, such modern pronouncements are in no way incompatible with the continuation of existing political practices. Above and

---

[6] For a development of this point, see Jean-Pascal Daloz, 'Le temps mondial au sud du Sahara: des représentations à la ressource politique' in Zaki Laïdi (ed.), *Le temps mondial* (Brussels: Editions Complexe, 1997).

beyond the need to espouse the rhetoric of profound policy changes, to which long-suffering Africans responded at first with enthusiasm, there is doubt whether the new (and even possibly radical) beliefs reflect actual reforms within the given political order on the continent. Is such new discourse not to be seen primarily from the instrumental perspective of appearing receptive to post-Cold War international orthodoxy?[7] It is indeed our view that ideology has been of secondary importance in Africa, where the logic of politics has commonly been driven by the need to acquire the patrimonial means of one's political legitimacy.[8]

Our argument is that it is the decline in the resources available for patronage rather than dissatisfaction with the patrimonial order *per se* which has undermined the legitimacy of political elites on the continent. Unable to satisfy the demands of their supporters, the Big Men on whom African regimes rely have been challenged by new pretenders. However, because the basis of politics remains grounded in a logic of clientelistic reciprocity, the number of plausible new contenders remains limited – hence the continued appeal of those older figures who once did manage to satisfy their supporters. The limited renewal of political elites is thus very strong evidence that a certain notion of leadership remains fundamental in Africa.

On the nature of leadership: beyond ideology

Much current literature on contemporary Africa – from radical manifestos to World Bank recommendations – places a heavy emphasis on the need for political leaders to become more 'responsible' and to improve the efficiency of 'public governance'. According to this view, greater political control by Africa's 'citizens' would ensure a proper reform of the existing political order. For us, however, such arguments lack credibility because they neglect to take into account the fact that the nature of the relations between rulers and ruled is determined by practices which have little to do with the formal structure of power.

It is crucial to understand that the foundations of political accountability in Africa are both collective and extra-institutional: they rest on the particularistic links between Big Men, or patrons, and their constituent communities.[9] That is why politics on the continent is essentially factional. Here too there has been a tendency in

---

[7] One small example: two of Frederick Chiluba's sons are called Tito and Castro.

[8] Under the Second Republic in Nigeria some aspiring politicians did not hesitate to change party affiliation three times, with scant regard for those parties' political programmes.

[9] For a detailed analysis of an issue which is all too often treated simplistically, see Chabal, 1992, particularly Chapters 3, 8 and 10.

the latest analysis of recent political transitions to overestimate the extent to which the so-called process of 'democratization' has resulted in a fundamental political transformation. Above and beyond the expectations generated by multi-party elections, and even more by leadership or regime changes, it is far from clear that such transitions have in practice modified the complexion of political relations between the governors and the governed.

Indeed, the wholesale adoption of a political vocabulary issued from the Western democratic experience is eminently misleading: the words do not correspond to the realities which they are supposed to embody. In sub-Saharan Africa, prestige and influence are intimately linked to the number of one's clients (however loosely that may be defined). It is undoubtedly the recognition which they bestow upon their leaders (or patrons) that determines the latter's social standing and political status. Within such a context, they must at all times be seen to cater for those on whose support their political legitimacy rests. The sanction of electoral success only becomes operational when it is congruent with patrimonial politics.

That is why, despite the undeniably large gap (in terms of resources and lifestyle) between elites and populace, leaders are never dissociated from their supporters. They remain directly linked to them through a myriad of nepotistic or clientelistic networks staffed by dependent intermediaries.[10] A person of substance will increase his authority if his constituents identify with him: if he, in other words, incarnates their hopes and aspirations. To do so, however, is hard work. Abuses of power are tolerated so long as the patron is able to meet with adequate largesse the (insatiable) demands which are made upon his person.

It would be wrong, however, simply to interpret such relational political clientelism as mere manipulation on the part of autonomous factional leaders. Their exercise of power rests firmly on commonly recognized and mutually accepted terms. Political elites themselves must operate within well-defined constraints, even if patron-client relations remain unequally biased in their favour. Indeed, patrons can easily suffer what we would call 'the blackmail of the ruled', that is, the obligation of personalized and vertical redistribution to which they must submit in order to anchor their position across the different social strata which provide support. Recent sociological research on democracy and political culture in Zambia, for example, confirms that patron-client links continue to be fundamental. The populace expects to exchange

---

[10] Even in Zaire where Mobutu was acknowledged to have largely cut himself off from the population, redistributive networks reached relatively low down the social order, according to one of the foremost specialists on the country. See Williame, 1995.

political support for concrete help: that is the only way in which politics makes sense to them.[11]

What this means is that, despite the current political 'democratic transitions' on the continent, there has been no modification in the notion of representation – firmly anchored as it is in the patrimonial system discussed above. The understanding of the concept of citizenship and of the purpose of the individual vote remains indelibly linked to the anticipation of the direct communal (or even personal) benefit which elections offer. People tend to vote because they are expected, or 'asked', to do so, or perhaps because it is indispensable to be seen to be voting in a certain way. On the whole, they do not vote because they support the ideas, even less read the programmes, of a particular political party, but because they must placate the demands of their existing or putative patron.

The vote is not primarily a token of individual choice but part of a calculus of patrimonial reciprocity based on ties of solidarity. Elections thus provide opportunities for instrumental political competition. Multi-party elections do not in this respect change the fundamental rules of the game. Admittedly, they tend to make visible and more vocal the rivalry between various challengers which was previously obscured and muffled within the single-party political machine. Nevertheless, the process of legitimation which elections engender remains essentially the same. To pursue the Zambian example: however disappointed the northern backers of Frederick Chiluba and the MMD are, they continue to support their MPs and their president because they expect very little from the other parties, seen as representing the interests of competing ethnic and geographical communities.[12] This is also the view at the top. A Zambian minister was quoted as saying: 'If I don't appoint people from my own region, who else will?'[13]

This type of more realist analysis, which stresses the nature of vertical or personalized exchange, goes against most standard interpretations of politics on the continent. The developmentalist approach, for instance, simply takes for granted the ultimate Westernization of African societies. With the collapse of communist regimes, there has been renewed interest in a paradigm which now emphasizes, in a similarly narrow causal fashion, the developmental merit of economic liberalization and democratization. However, the weight of personalized and infra-institutional dynamics remains stronger and more consequential than any programme of reform artificially induced from out-

[11] See Jean-Pascal Daloz, 'Can we eat democracy?' in Daloz & Quantin, 1997.
[12] See interviews in the *Weekly Post* (8 February 1994).
[13] *New Africa* (June 1992).

side. The modalities of present multi-party forms of government may appear to have changed, the façade of the state may have been reshaped, but the real stuff of politics continues to be driven by the selfsame political logic.

It would be erroneous, therefore, to assume that sub-Saharan Africa is in the process of adopting Western-style democracy – that is, a system where, according to Schumpeter, the populace would 'produce a government free to govern unhindered until the next election'.[14] Politics in Africa simply cannot be encompassed within the significant but infrequent electoral process precisely because it is experienced and instrumentalized according to the short-term logic of representation and reciprocity. That is why there is also no discernible scope for the elaboration of a political and administrative sphere, a bureaucracy on the Western model, both professionally competent and autonomous from society.

The developmental approach is thus very largely ideological, since it assumes, simplistically, that what is happening on the continent is a 'pathological' deviation from the model. And yet the empirical observation of events in Africa gives no reason to suppose that present transitions have ushered in a new civic age where individual 'citizens' will express personal preferences based on a well-considered choice of alternative programmes. This explains why most studies on current transitions simply fail to account convincingly for the dynamics of contemporary politics in Africa. Furthermore, a focus on democratization runs the serious risk of deflecting attention from those more significant processes which we do need to understand in order to make sense of what is actually occurring on the continent.

Similarly, it will be readily seen that our view of the predominance of the informalization of politics goes against another influential approach, that which is based on a class analysis. Even if it is today acceptable to cast doubt on the existence of a *bona fide* bourgeoisie in Africa, much Africanist writing remains distinctly influenced by what we might call neo-Marxist, or 'Third World', approaches. What we mean is that there is a strong analytical strand in African studies which privileges an interpretation of the continent based on socio-economic and political cleavages. Ruling 'classes' and other assorted 'dictators' oppress the 'suffering masses' who, in their turn, seek to resist by all available means. However, the search for a form of class consciousness divorced from other overwhelmingly present types of self-identification (whether ethnic, religious, regional or factional) turns out to be elusive.

---

[14] Joseph Schumpeter, *Capitalism, Socialism and Democracy* (London: Allen & Unwin, 1976), Chapter XXII.

Indeed, if class is defined (in keeping with standard sociology) as a self-consciously constituted group organized to defend its economic interests and to assert those interests against other similar ensembles, then it is clear that the continent is largely devoid of social classes. That this is so is not surprising, as should be clear from the arguments we have presented so far in this book. Even if it had achieved the economic means of its hegemonic ambitions, any elite which became a ruling 'class', thus cutting itself from the rest of society, would rapidly lose prestige, influence and, thereby, legitimacy. Within the existing African political culture, patrons will always have closer links with their clients than with rival faction leaders. At the opposite end of the social scale, ordinary people will always relate more directly with their local Big Man than with their economic peers elsewhere in the country.

Leaving aside the question of class consciousness, it is debatable whether there are, objectively, real classes on the continent. Most Marxist or neo-Marxist analysts have had difficulty locating social classes in present-day Africa which might exhibit characteristics similar to their Western or Eastern counterparts. Some have resorted to the notion of 'class fraction' in order to explain divisions within what appeared to be relatively well-constituted economic interest groups (such as miners, railways workers or stevedores). The question of whether classes are currently beginning to emerge in Africa goes beyond the scope of the present discussion. On the basis of our research, however, we would merely conclude that the move from primordial solidarity to clientelistic coalition does not so far appear to have led to the type of class formation familiar to modern Western or Eastern societies.

In more general terms, therefore, we would argue that our approach casts doubt on any interpretation of African politics which postulates a radical cleavage between a minority elite and the rest of the population. Analysing politics from the perspective of our inquiry into the notion of leadership, the major question to be addressed is that of representation. To what extent does the population delegate, or entrust, power to its representatives?[15] Here, some writers have contended that the African elite is gradually becoming more autonomous, thereby progressively asserting hegemony over society. It is true that this elite has its own interests and that it is continuously seeking to acquire ever increasing resources by all available means, including predatory. In our view, however, it would be misleading to believe that it does so as an autonomous and all-powerful 'class', whose interests would be economically and politically antagonistic to those of the other social groupings.

Our approach emphasizes instead the extent to which relations between leaders and followers, rulers and ruled, are to be understood

---

[15] See Geraint Parry, *Political Elites* (New York: Praeger, 1970).

in terms of asymmetrical reciprocity. Indeed, the imperative of gifts and gift-giving remains central to social life in contemporary Africa: it is more important to give, and thus to earn credit with others, than to receive. That is why gifts accepted are so frequently offered instantly to someone else. We are not, of course, arguing that such relations of reciprocity reduce the extremes of social wealth and status to be found in Africa. We are merely saying that they make such inequalities more legitimately bearable than they would otherwise have been, which also means that even the lowliest client can expect to benefit from his affiliation to a patron. The truly destitute are those without patrons.

Our argument thus casts serious doubts on the validity of those interpretations which conceive of African societies from an excessively dichotomized view, emphasizing divisions between 'high' and 'low' politics, elites and masses, ruling classes and populace. Such is decidedly not the reality on the continent. On the contrary, what we observe empirically is not an opposition between extremes but relative continuity – which binds the local to the national. Unequal reciprocity is akin to a trickle-down effect where resources flow downwards from the top in exchange for a recognition of the status and power of the provider. For those at the very bottom of the social order, the material prosperity of their betters is not itself reprehensible so long as they too can benefit materially from their association with a patron linking them to the elites.

This aspect of leadership is perhaps best illustrated by the extraordinary levels of ostentation found throughout Black Africa. It is common on the continent to notice the greatest displays of luxury in an environment of poverty and squalor, most particularly in the urban areas. Magnificent mansions sit square in the middle of slum areas. Gleaming white limousines make their way down dank and filthy alleyways. Prosperously rotund businessmen mingle readily with dishevelled and dirty children. Remarkably, there appear to be few outward signs of resentment, envy, even less aggression, vis-à-vis such blatant, and apparently callous, displays of wealth. On the contrary, what is noticeable is the extent to which the less fortunate show their appreciation of the manifestation of ostentation on show, as though it reflected well on them. Wealth thus revealed appears, indirectly, to be a symbol of their *collective prominence*, according to a process which we identify as 'vertical symbolic redistribution'.

This may explain not only why ostentation is not objectionable to the majority of the population concerned but how it is intrinsic to the existing socio-political order. Not to display wealth opulently would be tantamount to an admission of low collective self-esteem. Ostentation is thus an integral part of the process of representation, understood here in its three dimensions: showing (off), embodying the qualities and affirming the ambitions, of a given community. Dependants expect that their patrons will exhibit their status and assert their rank by means of the visible attributes of material possessions. Magnificence is understood here as munificence. Ostentation is, therefore, not primarily seen, either by patrons or clients, as the self-gratifying pastime of the elite (as it most often is in the West) but corresponds to the widespread expectation of the populace. What is spent on prestige is not resented unless it is seen to be blatantly to the detriment of those who would otherwise count on benefiting from such accumulation of wealth. Those who disburse wisely on their dependants can indulge the extremes of conspicuous consumption. Ostentation will then merely serve to enhance their prestige and the legitimacy of their 'representativeness'.

Some analysts are wont to emphasize that ruling classes ultimately develop the ideology (in terms of the false consciousness) required by their socio-economic standing. If that is the case, we need to explain why conceptions of ostentation are widely shared by both rulers and ruled, dominators and dominated, 'high' and 'low' society. Indeed, the examination of the behaviour of rising elites is instructive. Their economic success does not seem to affect their demeanour in the way class analysis would predict. The nouveaux riches do not cut themselves off from their original community. On the contrary: they will readily be seen having a drink and conversing with their former friends and relatives.

To be sure, they will spend conspicuously, buying expensive designer clothes or luxury cars and showing themselves off with pretty women. But they will continue to live in their own area, where typically they will build the most impressive home they can afford. They will receive, entertain and help their friends and neighbours: in short, they will begin to gather clients. So long as the newly rich are perceived to behave appropriately as patrons, they will be respected and admired, becoming in this way role models. As such, the accumulation of wealth is inherently linked to a notion of legitimacy which undermines the expected dynamics of class formation.

Our research on contemporary Africa indicates that present political transitions have not hitherto changed either the role of the elites or the nature of leadership. It is true that many regimes have suffered dramatic losses of legitimacy but this is more often than not due to a decline in the resources they have available for (re)distribution. It is the economic crisis rather than the method of government which has weakened political elites on the continent. Conversely, there is little evidence that the emergence of new leaders (like Chiluba or Kabila) has changed the social framework of reciprocity which characterizes African politics. Interpreting present political transitions as being the result of the strong 'democratic mobilization' of the populace against existing ruling elites appears to us to be wide of the mark. Most people are primarily worried about their everyday living conditions and are more concerned about finding new patrons (or old recycled elites) than about changing the complexion of the political order.

For us, therefore, the concept of leadership, a standard notion in political analysis, has the immense merit of stressing both the relational and the relative nature of the links between rulers, intermediaries and ruled. African politicians undoubtedly have both regional and national ambitions; they aim to 'represent' the largest and most diverse constituency possible. However, the strategy they have to follow is essentially patrimonial: they need to accumulate clients, building up their networks from the local to the national level. Because such political ambitions require substantial resources, there are few who can manage constantly and regularly to feed a complex of clients with national ramifications.

There is no reliable evidence that this type of particularistic leadership, based as it is on communal links and clientelistic transactions, is waning on the continent – although it might be markedly weakened by the dearth of resources which the elites currently suffer. On the contrary, we would argue that the present economic crisis in Africa reinforces, rather than undermines, the patrimonial political order, even if it makes possible some changes in political leadership. Without a wholesale mutation in existing political culture and mentalities, as well as a proper institutionalization of the state, elections are unlikely to alter the all-important logic of vertical and personalized patronage.

That this should be so is not such a remarkable conclusion from either the historical or comparative perspective. What may appear to be an 'exotic' aspect of African politics has in fact been a common form of political transaction in the world during earlier periods. Indeed, there are still today many societies (for example, in the Middle East) where patronage forms an essential part of politics. It is in reality the Western trajectory, characterized by the development of the modern legal and rational state, the emergence of individualism and the assertion of class identities, which is startlingly distinct. The African informal political order as we have sought to present it in the first part of this volume is thus a system grounded in a reciprocal type of interdependence between leaders, courtiers and the populace. And it is a system that *works*, however imperfectly, to maintain social bonds between those at the top and bottom of society. How it works, and what its limits are, is what we discuss in the next two sections of the book.

II

The 'Re-traditionalization' of Society

This second part of our book moves away from the more classical political issues to examine those which are usually associated with social analysis and anthropology. Here we want to focus our attention more specifically on the individuals and communities which form society. We do so, however, from a wholly political perspective, by which we mean that what interests us is the ways in which questions of society impinge on the political life of African countries today. What are, for example, the boundaries of politics in contemporary Africa? How do these boundaries differ from those in the West? To what effect?

We start from the observation that much of what is happening in contemporary Africa seems to reinforce the notion that the continent is moving 'backwards' – that it is in some ways 're-traditionalizing'. What is meant here, at an immediate and relatively superficial level, is that what we see in Africa confounds expectations of modernization. Both the ways in which Africans appear to define themselves and the manner in which they behave fail to conform to what social scientists expect of societies which are modernizing.

Although the most internationally visible indicator of such 're-traditionalization' is the apparent resurgence of ethnicity and its attendant 'tribal' politics and violence, there are many other areas which seem to defy our experience. Among these, the most salient are perhaps the lasting differences in self-identity between Africans and Europeans, the growing importance of African religions, the continued significance of witchcraft, the expansion of criminal activities and the increasing resort to extreme and, often, ritualized violence in situations of civil disorder.

Taken together these questions raise the issue of modernization. Can societies which exhibit such features be modern, or even modernizing? Is it the case that the current African crisis has actually unleashed on the continent a regression, a movement backwards? Are such features of present African societies an indication that Africans are less likely than others to become the individuals and citizens which are deemed necessary to the development of truly politically modern, economically successful and technologically advanced countries?

Our discussion of the 're-traditionalization' of Africa leads on from our analysis, in Part I, of the very foundations of the present political order on the continent. It emphasizes the extent to which Africans operate on several different registers – from the most visibly modern to the most ostensibly traditional – in their everyday lives. The failure to understand the apparently contradictory nature of politics in Africa is itself very largely the result of an analytical convention which tends to assume a paradigmatic dichotomy between the realms of the modern and of the traditional. The African elites, however, operate in a world which combines both, a world congruent with the beliefs of the rest of the population. Thus, our own analysis seeks to shed light on a process of modernization which contains such strong elements of 're-traditionalization' as to make the prospect of Westernization as we understand it very problematic.

The question of identity – of which ethnicity forms a large part – is central to our comprehension of African societies. Classical political analysis rests on a notion of the discrete, autonomous and self-referential individual which does not seem relevant to Africa. Much as modernization theory has sought indications that Africans were moving in the direction of the Westernized individual, the reality remains obdurately different. Most Africans are today no nearer being similar to North Americans than they were in the 1960s. Is this because they have failed to 'develop' or is it, more realistically, because they are modernizing differently? Is not modernization in effect determined by the complex and contradictory ways in which social and cultural traditions evolve and are transformed, in Africa as elsewhere?

Similarly, we investigate the role of what we call here, with obvious and intended ambiguity, the 'irrational'. Juxtaposing, as we do, witchcraft and religion indicates clearly that the analysis of the use and abuse of the irrational requires an open mind about the political implications of the belief systems most relevant to Africans in their everyday life. We do not aim here to give an analytical account of this immensely complex and variegated question but merely to suggest the ways in which such belief systems affect the perception and conduct of politics – both at the micro- and macro-levels. In turn, these considerations are likely to help us make sense of how the so called 'irrational' affects the evolution of the continent.

Finally, we examine more closely the question of why the present African crisis has engendered such high levels of brutality and crime. Although it is generally the case that violence is an indication of difficult or rapid historical transitions, the question here is whether there is in Africa a specific, perhaps cultural, instrumentalization of the illicit which affects the ways in which the business of politics is conducted. Are there 'entrepreneurs' of crime and makers of war whose influence on the informalization of politics is such as to make the instrumentalization of disorder the main economic resource on the continent? To what extent is the illicit legitimate? Furthermore, is there a discernible new form of political violence which is shaping the evolution of African societies – as might be suggested by the recent events in countries like Liberia and Rwanda? What does this mean for Africa's future?

4

Of Masks & Men | The Question of Identity

One of the central issues in the political sociology of Africa is the question of whether the nature of identity – meaning both self-identity and the perception of the identity of others – over-determines the political condition of the continent. In particular, there is continuing debate about the place of ethnicity – which, far from having become less salient, as modernization theory had led us to believe, has seemingly become the crucible of African politics. Is this to be explained primarily by contingent factors, such as a recourse to ties of familiarity in times of crisis, or is it to be seen as an indication that the notion of the individual is distinct? How do we reconcile what is happening in Africa with our view of social development?

The question of modernity is at the heart of our appreciation of the nature of identity in the African context. The belief that modernization is predicated on the development of a particular form of identity – broadly Westernization – has affected our perception of what is happening in Africa today. Our analysis of politics on the continent has often rested on falsely dichotomized perceptions of African identities. We have either tended to think of Africans in terms of a 'universal' notion of citizenship, whose sense of (political) identity would in due course conform to that of the West. Or we have been inclined to see Africans as entirely dissimilar, other: individuals whose 'traditional' notion of self made 'modern' politics virtually impossible.[1]

---

[1] It might be added here that Africans have been perennially adept at manipulating to their own ends our dichotomized perceptions – presenting themselves, according to circumstances, either as 'African' or 'modern', as seemed most instrumentally useful.

But our dilemma has been largely self-inflicted. It is our own narrow view of modernity which has constrained our understanding of
African identities. We have confused development and Westernization, thus making it difficult to grasp the singularity of what is
taking place on the continent in terms of modernization. Not only have
we been prone to explaining current events in Africa as a process of
'backwardness', but we have been slow to understand the complex
ways in which political change is taking place in Africa. Our failure,
for example, to explain satisfactorily why current 'democratic transitions' are not having the effects widely anticipated in the West, or our
difficulty in making sense of distinctly unorthodox political changes
in countries such as Uganda or Ethiopia, points to the limits of a
political analysis grounded on a notion of modernity which is simply
inadequate.

It is difficult to conceive of what a non-Western, particularly
'African', path to modernization is, both because we live in a Western
world and because, historically, the West modernized first.
Nevertheless, it is useful to remind ourselves that there are today a
(growing) number of modern, economically dynamic and scientifically
sophisticated countries, such as Japan and the other Asian 'tigers', following their own distinct development path. Indeed, their very
progress has sometimes been explained in culturalist terms, so that at
this stage we might simply define modernization as the ability to function and compete in the contemporary world, according to the economic and technological norms of the West.

In this chapter we approach the question of identity by focusing
attention on two key political issues. The first has to do with the ways
in which the political systems established at independence have been
Africanized.[2] The second discusses the instrumental role of ethnicity
in the construction of the modern African nation-state.

The meanings of Africanization

Much of our difficulty in understanding the peculiarities of African
politics lies with our expectations of what ought to have happened in
the post-colonial period – much of that a product of the assumptions
of modernization theory. More specifically, our view of how political
systems would operate after independence was largely determined by
our notions of Western identity. And indeed, the belief that parliamentary democracy would work in African countries rested on the
tenet that Africans would in time 'evolve' into identifiable citizens –

[2] For a systematic discussion of the question of the Africanization of politics, we
refer to Chabal 1992, Chapter 12.

that is, discrete individuals socialized into the ways of recognizing electoral forms of multi-party representation as a necessary *and* sufficient means of political accountability.

What happened after independence was the Africanization of politics, that is, the adjustment of imported political models to the historical, sociological and cultural realities of Africa. This is still going on today: the so-called democratic transitions are being reinterpreted locally. The dialectical process between the modernization of African forms of identity and the administration of political systems issued from the West has been complex, painful and chaotic. Moreover, it is taking place against the background of a severe economic crisis, which in its turn brings (through structural adjustment) further political conditionalities. As elsewhere, so in Africa, it is natural in times of crisis to turn to one's most familiar and reassuring beliefs about oneself and others.

The consequence of this process has been a transformation of existing forms of identity into individual and collective strategies for the management of change and disorder. Africans can no more rely on what we tend to see as their 'age-old' traditions than they can depend on the types of identity inherited from their colonial experience or gleaned since from their perception of a 'post-modern' Western world (the Eastern socialist option having proved all too ephemeral). They cast themselves as mobile phone-wielding businessmen while keeping contact with the village spirits. They reinterpret Rambo from the memory of their initiation ceremonies.

That this should be so is not surprising. Indeed, another error would consist in wanting to identify, as it were, 'the' African notion of identity – as futile a task as it would be for Europe. There is no fixed unchanging identity on the continent – traditional or otherwise. The kernel of our argument is that we should analyse African identities as they change over time and as they are instrumentalized politically. In so doing, however, we need to be particularly mindful of those important sociological and cultural characteristics which matter to Africans today. It is not a question of making some vague generalization on a form of African identity but, more simply, a matter of observing carefully everyday political facts in their variegated manifestations.

Among those facts which we believe are important to an understanding of the politics of the African identity, we want to explore more specifically the following: the boundaries of politics; the notion of the individual; the issue of political legitimacy; the question of representation; and the meaning of political opposition.

(a) The boundaries of politics. We must recognize first that in Africa the boundaries of politics contrast significantly from those prevailing in Western political systems. Whereas in the West politics is predicated on a well-defined separation between, on the one hand, the political realm and, on the other hand, the more economic, social, religious or cultural areas, this is clearly not the case in Africa. We cannot assume that we know what is or is not 'political'. On the contrary, we need to analyse how the very perception of what is political impinges on actual political practice.

Partly because African identities incorporate a communal notion of the individual, the vision of politics is both more inclusive and more extensive than it is in the West. It is more *inclusive* in that it contains the multiple aspects of the relationship between individual and community that we outline below, so that, for example, the fact that a person belongs to a particular village or age group may have significance for some political activities. It is more *extensive* in that it projects with varying degrees of intensity into the other realms of human existence: social, economic, religious, cultural, etc., so that, for instance, the occult remains of immediate practical relevance to the conduct of politics in Africa today.

The boundaries of politics are also porous: politics is seen legitimately to include many other, less obviously political, activities. Perhaps the most fluid in this respect is that which links political and economic enterprise. In Africa, it is expected that politics will lead to personal enrichment just as it is expected that wealth will have direct influence on political matters. Rich men are powerful. Powerful men are rich. Wealth and power are inextricably linked. In other words, the reality of politics in Africa is that, in this respect as in many others, there is no rigidly recognizable boundary defining its limits with regard to wealth. The political realm overlaps extensively with all the other spheres of profitable human activity, from the religious to the commercial. Consequently, and crucially, there has not emerged in Africa the kind of differentiated political realm which is the foundation of politics in the West.

(b) The notion of the individual. Western political systems are based on a concept of the citizen which appears of little relevance to Africa. Not only do Africans not conceive of themselves as discrete individuals in the Western mould, but few would accept that their own identity as citizen could be circumscribed politically as it is in the West. The notion of the individual in Africa, with due allowance for the differences found in various parts of the continent, is again one which is inclusive rather than exclusive. In other words, individuals are not perceived as being meaningfully and instrumentally separate from the (various) communities to which they belong.

This means that the individual remains firmly placed within the family, kin and communal networks from which (s)he is issued. Whatever social changes have taken place in post-colonial Africa have not (so far at least) resulted, as they have in the West, in the gradual but seemingly permanent erosion of the communal in favour of the individual.[3] Africans do not now appear to feel that their 'being modern' requires them to be single individuals whose life choices are essentially determined by their own private circumstances and desires. Difficult as it may be for us to conceive of modernity other than in our own terms, it is necessary to understand how Africans can be both modern and 'non-individual(ist)' if we are to make sense of political events on the continent.[4]

The boundaries between the individual and the communal in Africa are thus porous – or at least not as firm as in the West – in ways which are politically significant. Indeed, the very term – an individual – is in this respect a misnomer, for it implies a distance from the community which simply does not exist. Furthermore, the notion of the individual as it applies in Africa has a profound bearing on the question of identity. Where the individual and communal remain subjectively so intertwined, personal identities will necessarily reflect a degree of collective (kin, clan, ethnic, etc.) concerns which may easily appear to be inimical to the development of what we see as 'modern' society. We thus need to explain African politics on a conceptual basis which differs radically from that which underpins Western political theory.

(c) The issue of legitimacy. Such differences on the boundaries of politics, the place of the individual and the role of the citizen quite obviously impinge upon the key issue of what is, or is not, politically legitimate. The difficulty we have in understanding politics in Africa stems partly from our poor grasp of the very question of legitimacy. From the perspective of Western political theory, we are bound to consider that the greater part of what passes for politics is clearly outside 'legitimate' bounds. And yet our research on African politics has revealed that this is not necessarily how ordinary Africans feel. Unless we understand fully what is politically legitimate (and why) we run the risk of permanently misreading political events. Much of what is deemed criminalization, as we discuss in Chapter 6, is not perceived as illegitimate, even if it often is illegal.

There is, clearly, a temptation to interpret the crisis of the post-colonial state in Africa from the Western viewpoint of the failure of modern politics. It is more fruitful, however, to try to understand the extent to which the Western model inherited at independence has

[3] 'Seemingly' because there is evidence in Europe that we may have reached the limits of this process of 'individualization'; there now appear to be moves to recreate a stronger sense of community – whatever that, in practice, might mean.

[4] Whether a process of sharper economic development would induce, as it is claimed it now does in Asia, a greater degree of individualism is an open and, for the moment, moot question.

been reconstructed by the Africanization of the notion of political legitimacy. If, for example, the communal or ethnic bias of members of the government is considered desirable, then the consequences of such bias in terms of governmental efficiency may well be acceptable to the majority of the population. If, similarly, it is considered desirable that politicians should become Big Men, then the (political) means by which they acquire the wealth to sustain such status may well also be regarded as legitimate. To say this, however, is not to say (as one might easily be tempted to) that there is no limit to how ethnically biased or wealthy politicians can become. Unjustified excesses are clearly perceived as illegitimate.

Consequently, our difficulty in making sense of African politics is, in part at least, a result of our inability to conceptualize the question of legitimacy. It is easier to be simplistic and categorical on this issue than to try to understand the extent to which the behaviour of political elites, as analysed in Chapter 3, may or may not appear to be legitimate in the eyes of their various possible constituencies. Thus, for example, although to the untrained Western eye both Houphouët-Boigny and Mobutu may have appeared to share the features commonly associated with megalomaniac tyrants, there is no doubt that in reality the former could boast a degree of political legitimacy (in the full sense of the word) that the latter never possessed. And this for the simple reason that Houphouët-Boigny remained for most of his political career[5] within the boundaries of what was broadly acceptable to the majority of his constituencies. The same distinction holds true between Kenyatta, who had widespread support, and Arap Moi, who is now perceived by most Kenyans to have overstepped the boundaries of the legitimate.

(d) The question of representation. There is in contemporary Africa an understanding of representation which, again, does not fit easily within the Western model. Where the notion of the individual and the meanings of legitimacy are so distinct, it is inevitable that the perception of what makes for 'representativeness' will also be singular. Whereas in our Western democracies the function of the representative is both to act on behalf of (all the citizens of) a given constituency and to legislate in parliament in the national interest, in Africa the situation is infinitely more complex. This is because the identity of the representative is as important a consideration as the multifarious role which representation entails. It is also because all politicians, whether elected locally or nationally, are expected to act as the spokespeople and torchbearers of their community.

---

[5] At least until the construction of the largest Catholic cathedral in the world in his home town of Yamassoukro.

Put at its simplest, representation in Africa is necessarily communal or collective. The legitimacy of the representative is thus a function of the extent to which s(he) embodies the identities and characteristics of the community. It means, inevitably, that a representative must be a member of that community – in ethnic as well as, perhaps, religious, regional or professional terms. It implies further that s(he) must be seen to incarnate the real (or even imaginary) qualities and virtues of the community which s(he) seeks to represent. What matters here is less the degree to which the candidate reflects the views and opinions of the electorate than the extent to which the selected person is a worthy embodiment of that community – obviously in terms of its own self-perception. Hence a Bamiléké representative in Cameroon would be expected to be a successful example of this thriving business community.

Similarly, the role of the representative in Africa does not easily conform to the Western norm, for its primary attribute is the defence and furtherance of communal interests rather than the elaboration of the national well-being. This means that representation quite literally entails the active improvement of the material condition of the community represented, on the easily verifiable assumption that all other officials will act in the same way. In effect, the legitimacy of representation hinges very largely on the extent to which the elected candidate (whether member of the government or of the legislature) manages to demonstrate success in obtaining for the community resources which it would not otherwise receive. This instrumental notion of representation may not be the most amicable to that of the maximization of the common good but it is the norm and one, therefore, which political analysis must take into consideration.

(e) The meaning of political opposition. It follows, therefore, that in Africa the notion of political opposition has a different significance. Whereas in the West, the practice of democratic elections is, with the exception of coalition governments, a zero-sum game – there are recognizable winners and losers, each with a proper constitutional role – the same cannot apply in Africa. If the notion of the individual and the meaning of representation are bound up with the identity, defence and furtherance of the interests of the community, then there can be no place in the political system for an opposition with no means of delivering resources to its constituents. To be in opposition is of no intrinsic or even political value. Politics in this respect cannot be a zero-sum game. Or if it is, the political system becomes inherently unstable, even illegitimate.

Although this question of political opposition may appear to be narrowly technical, it is at the very heart of the present politics of Africa. We would argue that it is the single most important reason why the so-called democratic transitions on the continent have failed to generate the establishment of stable political systems. Democracy, in its (Western) multi-party winner-take-all guise, simply has no proper role for electoral losers in Africa. Or rather, its constitutionally defined role is both unworkable in the context of weak parliamentary systems and contrary to the legitimate expectations which voters have of their representatives. For this reason, if for no other, there has been widespread disillusionment with 'democratic' political systems on the continent.

The reality of contemporary Africa is that the pragmatically and symbolically instrumental function of politics is critical. Politicians are expected to represent their constituents properly, that is, to deliver resources to them. It is, therefore, comprehensively useless to be an opposition politician if the opposition has no access to the means which its members need and expect. The only conceivable democratic political system which could fulfil the present requirements would be one which would not be a zero-sum game: for example, a form of proportional representation which would give both power and access to resources on the basis of electoral success. As this is unlikely to happen, it is understandable why, in contemporary Africa, opposition is often seen only as a strategy to secure co-optation into the ruling circles.

Imagined ethnicities

Ethnicity is commonly considered in Africanist circles as a problem: either because it is seen as an inconvenient leftover from a previous 'traditional' age and a hindrance to modernization or else because it is viewed as a divisive political weapon used by unscrupulous political operators. Both these views, however, are themselves throwbacks to mechanistic interpretations of African realities, casting ethnicity as a simplistically 'tribalist' form of identity or as a mere tool. We need to conceptualize ethnicity as a dynamic, multi-faceted and interactive cluster of changeable self-validated attributes of individual-cum-collective identities. There is no 'single' ethnicity out there cast in stone for ever. There are ways of defining oneself and others in accordance with a set of beliefs, values and subjective perceptions which are both eminently malleable and susceptible to change over time.

We all have an ethnicity. In the West, it is normally subsumed under citizenship, though, as in the Basque region of Spain, there are exceptions. In Africa such sentiments are usually more salient and more consequential because of the nature of the evolution of contemporary African politics. What it is important to distinguish conceptually is the notion of ethnicity from its political instrumentalization. Why and how ethnicity is instrumentalized politically is conditioned by present historical circumstances, in Africa as anywhere else. There is more, however. Given the lack of congruence in post-colonial Africa between political identities and the model of the modern nation-state inherited at independence and to which all regimes claim to be committed, is it not possible that ethnicity could furnish the foundations of an African nation-state? Is modernity, in other words, necessarily at the expense of ethnicity?

The argument that is beginning to emerge is that ethnicity has been misinterpreted, both historically and conceptually. In historical terms, there is now ample evidence of what has been called the 'invention of ethnicity', by which is meant the ways in which it was constructed and instrumentalized during the colonial period. There is, of course, no denying the fundamental impact which colonization had on the configuration and reconfiguration of ethnic identities, although it is quite clear that such effect was distinct in every region and impinged differently on existing or imaginary 'tribal' perceptions. It is not possible, therefore, to assert an 'iron law' on the construction of ethnicity under colonial rule. The effects were simply too diverse. What it is possible to say, however, is that the emphasis on the colonial role's 'invention' has frequently been at the expense of the more general analysis of the political significance of ethnicity in contemporary Africa.

Indeed, what should be understood by the invention of ethnicity is not that such affiliations did not exist prior to colonial rule but simply that they were reconstructed during that period according to the vagaries of the interaction between colonial rule and African accommodation. What matters historically, then, is not so much the colonial roots of today's ethnic groups but the deeper processes by which their sedimentation took place, from pre-colonial times to the present, so that, for example, it is more important to understand how the present-day ethnicity of Hutu or Kikuyu evolved over time than it is to demonstrate that these ethnic groups were 'created' during the colonial period. The fact that some ethnic groups were more creatively invented during colonial rule than others does not in and of itself make them any more or less genuine, or legitimate, than others.

Historically, then, we may consider the construction of modern ethnicity in much the same light as we regard that of nationality in Europe. Invented ethnicities are, from such a perspective, no different from imagined communities; indeed, they are imagined communities.[6] What is significant in Africa, and differs from the process by which the European nation-state evolved, is that the invention of modern ethnicity was coincidental in time with the imposition on the continent of the colonial political structure – itself ostensibly modelled on the European state. So that it was the colonial state which formalized the ethnic map and conspired to define the relationship between ethnicity

[6] See here Anderson, 1983.

and politics – both of which influenced directly the complexion of post-colonial polities. What has happened since independence, has been the working through of the practical consequences of the colonial 'politicization' of invented ethnicities.[7]

Conceptually, the notion of ethnicity has been excessively reified, meaning that it has all too often been studied at one remove from the question of identity – as we have shown above. Ethnicity is not an essentialist attribute of the African, but more simply one of several components of identity. Furthermore, it is not to be discussed outside its precise historical, and even geographical, context. For instance, to say that one was a Hutu student in Brussels in 1991 is not the same as to say that one was a Hutu journalist working at Radio Mille Collines in 1994 – since in the first instance the consequence of that statement was nil, whereas in the second, it contributed to the genocidal frenzy which resulted in the death of several hundred thousand Tutsis.

The political significance of ethnicity is thus almost wholly a function of the circumstances in which the question of such an affiliation becomes more salient. And, except in the most extremely polarized cases (such as Rwanda or Burundi), ethnicity is only one of the many possible forms of identity which mark out the politics of a particular historical period. Ethnicity, like nationality, can become politically salient at times, but it does not mean that it is, *per se* and at all times, the only significant aspect of African identity. Under different circumstances, other factors (such as profession, locality, religion or race) could, and indeed do, become politically more prominent, as we suggested in Chapter 2 in respect of Nigeria.

The question to be explored here, following Lonsdale's pioneering work,[8] is whether ethnicity could be or become the foundation myth, the ideology, of the modern African nation, much as nationalism was in Europe. Is it conceivable that, despite the apparent multiplicity of ethnic groups in Africa, a political compact based on ethnicity could bring together, rather than separate, the constituent members of what now form existing African countries? Could there be an 'ethnic state' instead of a nation-state? However severely artificial such an idea may appear to be, the experiment in ethnic politics currently taking place in Ethiopia suggests that it could be time to think differently about the place of ethnicity in the political evolution of Africa. Indeed, given the level of violence at present visited on so many Africans in the name of ethnicity, it might well be argued that there is no alternative to the

---

[7] See here Ekeh, 1990.
[8] See Lonsdale's two key chapters (11 and 12) on the Kikuyu, in Berman and Lonsdale, 1992, Book 2, as well as Lonsdale, 1996.

notion that ethnicity, as Lonsdale suggests, could become the corner-stone of more accountable political systems.

When does, in Lonsdale's view, ethnicity become political tribalism? The answer lies in the context of modern power struggles. This much is clear. But where Lonsdale innovates is in his demonstration of the historically complex nature of the moral economy of Kikuyu political thought at a time of acute political crisis (the Mau Mau rebellion). Above and beyond the intricate and subtle discussion of the contradic-tions in distinct notions of Kikuyu identity which Mau Mau revealed, what is most intriguing about the author's work is the manner in which he outlines what we might call the politically constructive role of eth-nicity. He writes (Berman and Lonsdale, 1992, Book 2:

> Political tribalism flows down from high-political intrigue; it con-stitutes communities through external competition. Moral ethnicity creates communities from within through domestic controversy over civic virtue ... it is the only language of accountability that most Africans have; it is the most intimate critic of the state's ide-ology of order. But moral ethnicity is not given its due in analyses of modern Africa; political tribalism, often called clientelism, is accorded too much explanatory sway, perhaps because it makes fewer demands on evidence... (p. 466)
>
> Moral ethnicity may not be an institutionalized force; but it is the nearest Kenya has to a national memory and a watchful politi-cal culture. Because native, it is a much more trenchant critic of the abuse of power than any Western political thought; it imagines freedom in laborious idioms of self-mastery which intellectuals too easily dismiss...
>
> Neither political tribalism nor moral ethnicity will disappear. They are two sides of the worldwide politics of cultural pluralism. Tribalism remains the reserve currency in our markets of power, ethnicity our most critical community of thought. Ethnic national-ism has been mobilized rather than disarmed by modern states, no matter whether liberal or authoritarian. The universal question becomes, then, how to save multicultural politics from the fearful minority domination of barren factional bargains that suppress productively principled argument... (p. 467)
>
> Inside every united tribe a debated ethnicity is struggling to get out. More public awareness of common ethnic predicaments might sometimes deter high-political resort to the auction room of tribalism ... Deep debates are suppressed by high faction. They could, if heard, lead to argument on the accountability of state power. To give them voice one must, at the least, lend an ear to alternative pasts. (p. 468)

The implications of Lonsdale's argument are clear: it is political trib-alism that suppresses the politically constructive role moral ethnicity could play in African politics. For Lonsdale, ethnicity, far from being a perennial cause of strife and division, potentially forms the basis of the moral social contract which could begin to force accountability on state power. This is an original and powerful argument. Original in that few European Africanists have ever provided more systematic evidence of the subtle role of ethnicity in African political thought. Powerful in that it suggests, contrary to thirty years of Africanist social science, that ethnicity will need to find proper expression if accountability is to return to the post-colonial political order in Africa. Political tribalism may be the bane of Africa but this is so, according to Lonsdale, only because the holders of state power have managed hitherto to silence the voice of what he calls moral ethnicity – not because ethnicity is in itself a force for darkness and destruction.

Ethnicity, then, like its counterpart, nationality, cannot be taken merely as that peculiar attribute of identity which becomes the principal source of divisions between neighbouring social groups. As Lonsdale sees it, it must also be construed as the foundation of an African 'indigenous' political thought – because, like nationality it is the repository of both culture and history. To say this, of course, is not to say that ethnicity would be the sole such foundation – a thought that would no doubt comfort the holders of 'tribalist' interpretations of Africa – but merely that it is central to the development of more accountable politics. The question of how, in practice, a political system based on moral ethnicity does not become, under the relentless pressure of the drive for power, the tyranny of political tribalism is one, however, that Lonsdale does not discuss. And yet it self-evidently is one of the most difficult issues for the political analyst. Is the possible transition from political tribalism to moral ethnicity anything other than wishful thinking? More crucially, is it not against the interests of those who benefit from the instrumentalization of disorder?

It has often been argued that Africa's post-colonial political problems have been caused by the imposition of a 'foreign' state, or political system, at independence.[9] This is not the way Lonsdale sees it. It is not the foreignness of the post-colonial state that is responsible for its excesses. Rather, it is that the structure of the post-colonial state has enabled those Africans who have held power to instrumentalize ethnicity into political tribalism in order to serve their patrimonial interests. In so doing they have suppressed a crucial aspect of their past and failed to create new, more impersonal, forms of accountability, which, in the present context, would obviously not be to their advantage.

Lonsdale's argument is not that Africa now needs 'to return' to its ancient, more indigenously democratic, past. It is one which deals with

[9] See here, for example, Basil Davidson, *The Black Man's Burden: Africa and the curse of the nation state* (London: James Currey, 1992).

Africa's present crisis as a crisis of modernity, leaving open the search for a viable model of politics. There has, of course, been no shortage of proponents of a return to pre-colonial roots, to some form of African 'authenticity', as a way of constructing a truly African political order. But we know to what end the Mobutus of Africa have used such a notion: 'authenticity' has more often than not been a smokescreen for the most blatant abuse of power. Political tribalism of that ilk, it is true, has not been confined to Africa, as the recent history of ethnic cleansing and tribal barbarity in the former Yugoslavia has amply confirmed. What is perhaps more specific to Africa is the extent to which political tribalism has become the common currency of modern politics.

The reasons for this are simple, if not cheering. Given that the African post-colonial political order has been essentially patrimonial and given the strong ethnic quality of African identity, African politicians have found it expedient to reduce ethnic politics to the lowest common tribal denominator. In a situation where political elites are primarily accountable to their own clients, the instrumental use of ethnicity is accepted as an integral part of legitimate politics. In times of crisis, however, such as virtually all African countries have entered since the 1980s, the situation changes. Where the elites are unable to uphold the political and economic basis of their legitimacy, they resort to more coercive and manipulative means, including overt political tribalism. The drift from the legitimate instrumental use of ethnicity to political tribalism is thus to be understood as part of the authoritarian deliquescence of political order in contemporary Africa, as it was in the former Yugoslavia.

The debate today, therefore, is whether Lonsdale is right in thinking that ethnicity can become the foundation myth of modern Africa or whether political modernity is only possible once the ethnic dimension is no longer as important to African identity as it currently is. Can a workable notion of national identity encompass a diversity of ethnic affiliations? Can there be ethnically based governmental institutions which function efficiently and for the common weal? Is an ethnic federal state viable? These are difficult questions but they will need to be addressed if we are to make any progress in the understanding of the relation between the fact of ethnicity and the potential operation of a putatively modern 'nation-state' in Africa.

An African scholar has recently reflected constructively on this issue. In a recent article, he upbraided francophone Africanists for their failure to conceptualize African politics other than in Eurocentric terms.[10] His view is that the two dominant paradigms of the post-colonial African state – one stressing the adaptation of the

---

[10] Mwayila Tshiyembe, 'La science politique africaniste et le statut théorique de l'État Africain: un bilan négatif', *Politique Africaine*, 71 (October 1998).

imported model, the other the neo-patrimonial conversion of the European state – neglect to take into account the centrality of ethnicity in the social and political imagination of most Africans. Like Lonsdale, then, Tshiyembe emphasizes the extent to which (moral) ethnicity is the foundation of African political thought.

Although the notion that ethnicity is fundamental to African identities is not new, what is fresh in both Lonsdale and Tshiyembe is the argument that ethnicity is creatively compatible with present African political modernity. The emphasis on ethnicity is not an argument about the 'backwardness' of African politics, but one about the necessary re-anchoring of African politics into its rightful history. Indeed, Tshiyembe's thesis is that since in Africa all countries (with a few exceptions, such as Lesotho or Swaziland) are multi-ethnic nations, the only appropriate political order is one which makes space for a political framework grounded in this multi-ethnic reality. In other words, politics must be based on, rather than avoid, the ethnic dimension of the present African nation-state. This is so, according to Tshiyembe, not primarily because of the essentialist ethnic condition of the African but because of the necessity of devising a political structure which is both legitimate in the eyes of the population and accountable in its operation. Whether the structure which he outlines is viable or not remains at this stage an open question.

5

**The Taming
of the Irrational**

Witchcraft
& Religion

To read about African life today is almost to be transported back a hundred years, when the newly established colonial powers 'revealed' to the world how backward Africa was, how much it needed to be civilized. Today, like yesterday, our perception is that Africans continue to be singularly superstitious: the occult is alive, witchcraft is thriving, ritual ceremonies abound, the link with the ancestors is as strong as ever and African religious communities are growing in strength. Not only does it appear that African societies are failing to become more secular, as they were widely expected to do, but there is a sense in which they are 're-traditionalizing' – in that the realm of the 'irrational'[1] is seemingly gaining in importance.

What is the political analyst to make of such facts? Are these manifestations of the strength of belief in the irrational merely an indication of the failure of Africa to modernize? How do we judge beliefs to be irrational? From what perspective do we assess the relation between modernity and the irrational? Are there reasons for thinking that the irrational is more important to politics in Africa than it is elsewhere? In which ways is the irrational instrumentalized politically?

Standard political analysis considers secularization – that is, the gradual diminution of the significance of the religious – as one of the key features of modernization. As societies 'develop', the political order is constructed on 'rational' rather than 'irrational' foundations and the practice of politics becomes increasingly dissociated from the world of religious beliefs. The realities of contemporary Africa, however, raise the question of how relevant such notions are on a conti-

---

[1] As it is used in this book, the notion of the irrational is merely an agreed codeword for religious belief in its broadest sense, not in any way a value judgement on the beliefs of Africans. We all have our realm of the irrational.

nent where modernity and the irrational appear to go hand in hand. Can we seriously understand what is happening in Africa unless we go beyond an analysis which considers the 'irrational' strictly from the perspective of the gradual secularization of modernizing societies? Do we not need to use an approach which will allow us to understand how the irrational may be compatible with a certain type of development which differs fundamentally from Westernization?

This chapter will attempt to throw light on some of these questions by elaborating a political analysis which helps to make sense of the realm of the so-called irrational. We look first at the nature of religious belief in the context of modernizing African societies. We then discuss how the uses of the irrational bear upon actual political practice on the continent. As in the previous chapter, we are not trying here to imply that there might be 'a' single type of irrational in Africa. We simply want to try to understand the extent to which the singularities of the religious beliefs to be found in Africa are relevant to its contemporary politics.

Belief

We need first to stress that our focus on what we call the irrational is not designed to imply that politics in Africa is not rational. Nor is it in any way to suggest that African religious beliefs are more irrational than others. For us, religious beliefs, beliefs in the irrational, are all the same. The question is how they matter politically. Is there a sense in Africa that belief in the irrational is manipulated by the elites for their own purposes? Or, conversely, is it the case that African elites, though often fully Westernized, share with the rest of the population a faith in the irrational which matters deeply to politics?

It is important to distinguish between two types of rationality. On the one hand, there is a more 'scientific' and universal rationality which forms the basis of technological progress. On the other, there is a more 'social' rationality which helps people to make sense of how they must live and interact within a given society. This is not, however, a distinction familiar to modernization theory since it merely assumes that these two forms of rationality are covalent and that they develop simultaneously. The most superficial examination of the experience of the Asian 'tigers' would suggest that this is obviously not the case. What interests us here, then, is to try to go beyond the simplistic assumption made by modernization theory that the irrational (usually taken to mean the 'traditional') necessarily withers with modernization.

For our purpose, the main question is the extent to which secularization is a prerequisite to political modernization or, to put it another way, whether modernization makes the business of politics less prone to the irrational. In the West, the irrational is meant simply not to be politically legitimate.[2] The modern democratic political framework, by way of a variegated process of political institutionalization, is supposed to have reduced the role of the irrational to the private sphere of the individual citizen. For example, politicians are not able explicitly to refer to the irrational (by which, again, we mean religious or occult beliefs) as a valid reason for their actions, even if many are clearly affected by such considerations.[3] But this is clearly not the case in Africa, where we know that the role of the irrational impinges, quite normally and legitimately, on all areas of human activity, including politics.

We want, in the first part of this chapter, to focus on four key aspects of religious belief in Africa which we think are particularly consequential for the continent's political culture: the boundary between the religious and the temporal; the pertinence of the religious to the notion of identity; the link between the living and the dead; and the relevance of the irrational to concepts of causality.[4]

(a) The religious and the temporal. A crucial feature of African belief systems is the absence of a firm boundary between the religious and the temporal. In Western political systems such a distinction is institutionalized and is critical to the functioning of the political order. In Africa, as elsewhere, politics is played out in a world which incorporates both and in which both have direct significance. While it is true that the African elite usually subscribe publicly to the Western separation between the irrational and the profane, there is ample evidence that their political behaviour is affected by religious beliefs which have overwhelming cultural weight. Indeed, it now seems clear – as is perhaps best shown in modern African fiction – that exposure to Western thought and education does not seriously reduce the degree to which the African educated elite continues to acknowledge the overlapping of the religious and the temporal.[5]

The world of overt politics is thus deeply influenced by the subterranean realm of the irrational. It is not just that politicians will seek the support of those with access to the religious and the occult, but

[2] Although the growing political influence of religious fundamentalist movements in the United States raises doubts as to how immune the American political system truly is to the appeal of the irrational.
[3] If both Ronald Reagan and Indira Gandhi consulted their astrologers, then who is to say which one of the two was more rational?
[4] We are, of course, aware that these four aspects do not remotely or adequately account for religious belief on the continent. Our aim is only to highlight some of the issues which we feel are most significant for politics.
[5] See, among many, Chinua Achebe, *The Anthills of the Savannah* (London: Picador, 1987).

that the decisions they make will be directly or indirectly influenced by these more covert considerations. It means, for example, that politicians readily use a political vocabulary (including the names by which they refer to themselves) liable to evoke in the minds of the population a link with the world of the irrational such as to endow them with special power.[6] There is here a topic for research which would probably yield more enlightening results than the perennial examination of political manifestos. Lonsdale's analysis of Kikuyu political thought is in this respect an example of the kind of work which helps directly to shed light on this poorly understood aspect of politics.[7]

It means too that politicians will be susceptible to pressures which are not easily accounted for by standard political analysis. Indeed, it is not possible to conceptualize African politics without paying due attention to the importance of the role of what, for want of a better word, must be called witchcraft. The relationship between witchcraft and power is discussed in detail below. Here we want only to stress the extent to which these considerations matter. Pressure comes in many guises, both external and self-generated. To take one example: in the political competition between 'traditional' leaders and modern politicians, the latter start at a disadvantage[8] in that they do not embody that combination of the secular and religious which carries immediate conviction. Much of their political behaviour can thus be explained by their attempt to acquire such attributes by paying proper heed to those who have access to the world of the irrational. Few, indeed, are African politicians who do not seek, in that sense, a 'religious' legitimacy, however secular their official discourse might be.

(b) The living and the dead. Central to African beliefs is the link between the world of the living and that of the dead. Of course, all religions offer both a rational mitigation for death and a method for coping with the apparently absolute break with those who have died. Established churches do so in a spiritual and symbolic way. African religions, however, do not conceive of a frontier between the living and the dead in the same way: all inhabit the same world. This means that religious conviction entails a belief in the presence and in the power of those who have departed – hence the prominence of the cult of the ancestors. Christian or Muslim Africans do not subscribe overtly to such

[6] See here the dossier in *Politique Africaine*, 64 (December 1996) on 'Démocratie: le pouvoir des mots'.

[7] John Lonsdale, Chapter 12, in *Unhappy Valley*, *op. cit.*

[8] They do, of course, have advantages which 'traditional' elites do not, such as control of a modern party machine and/or access to governmental resources. However, as we explain elsewhere, the distinction between modern and 'traditional' is not as meaningful as it might superficially appear to be.

rituals but may well, in private, hold on to the belief that the bond with the ancestors remains both real and significant.

One of the most important consequences of such belief is that, for Africans, there is a link between identity and locality which goes well beyond the Western notion of what the French call *terroir*. One's locality is where the ancestors are buried. It assumes, therefore, a significance which is more than symbolic – which is, in fact, instrumentally meaningful for the conduct of daily life. Obviously, Africans do move, or even migrate long distances, but they remain attached to a religious life that includes a distinct geographical centre. And, indeed, such a factor is one with a myriad political implications: from the simple one of local identity to the more complex influence which the relationship with the world of the dead may have on the behaviour of national political figures. Thus, the need of the wealthy to invest generously and to be buried in their village may well derive from a serious religious conviction and not just from sheer ostentation. Mobutu's compulsive decision to take the bones of his parents on his final journey into exile is exemplary in this respect.

Moreover, the universally recognizable tendency of politicians to favour their own may well have to do with more than mere ethnic bias. It may include a religious dimension which has hitherto almost never been taken into consideration but which could turn out to be deeply significant to the reality of politics in contemporary Africa. This is not to say that there may not be a whole range of sensible, practical, or expedient reasons for trusting one's kin rather than strangers. It is simply to point out that this particular aspect of religious African belief – the bond between the living and the dead – may well at times be of singular importance. We know that the dead must always be propitiated. We know too, for example, that politicians are often advised by masters of the occult who can access for them the spirits of the ancestors and summon their help.

(c) Identity and the irrational. We have already seen how, in Africa, the boundary between the individual and the community is infinitely more porous than it is in the West today. We need now to consider how the relationship between the two may be influenced by the nature of religious belief. The first point to note is that there is no clear-cut border between what we call religion (that is, the dogma of an established church) and witchcraft (meaning here belief in the occult). This entails continuity in the type and nature of belief in the irrational: Africans do not recognize a meaningful conceptual difference between what in the West would be identified as two different worlds, so that a Catholic teacher in a Central African mission school village is no more likely to dismiss or disregard witchcraft than is his uneducated and 'pagan' neighbour.

Secondly, the world of the irrational is one which binds the individual with the community in ways which are not open to choice. The nature of African religious belief is tied to a cult of the invisible world in which individual identity is constructed, in part at least, on the foundation of the communal ancestors. This is simply a fact of life, and not one open to discussion. Hence, very few Africans conceive of themselves other than in terms which link their own individuality with the collective identity of the community from which they originate. It is thus not simply a question of the ethnic dimension of personal identity but, perhaps more importantly, of the fact that such affiliation incorporates a religious dimension which is not given to change. This may explain, for example, why African politicians are always wary of offending the spirits of their home village.

Finally, we need to recognize that the notion of identity in Africa is one in which there is almost always place for the belief that the realm of the irrational can have direct and immediate practical influence on one's everyday life. It is a world with profane power of its own, power potentially stronger than human agency. That is why the irrational, or the occult, can be both an ally and an enemy and that the individual cannot afford not to be concerned with its putative significance. Established religions (Islam, Catholicism, etc.) can in some circumstances mitigate the weight of this concern, but only in rare cases are Africans totally secure in the belief that those universalist creeds can fully protect them. In some fundamental way, therefore, this faith in the power of the irrational is much more than a belief: it is part of the very fabric of the African psyche.

(d) Causality. The final aspect of the world of the irrational which it is worth considering is that which binds all the factors discussed above: the notion of causality. We know, if not well enough, that African religious thought incorporates a very strong emphasis on what causes are likely to explain those everyday events – accident, illness, death, sterility, failure, etc. – for which there is no immediate and obvious explanation. The very foundation of this religious world is the need to explain, to account for and thus to find the causality of that which is outside the relatively narrow and proximate domain of what is considered normal existence. We do not mean here to give a simplistic notion of what these processes are by dismissing them as 'ageless African practices'. We want to emphasize instead how important they are to contemporary religious belief and, perhaps more importantly, to suggest how they contribute to the notion of the 're-traditionalization' of African modernity.

African politics is influenced by the conceptions of causality which underpin ordinary life, notions which affect the meaning of responsibility and accountability. Whereas, in the West, politicians are held institutionally and politically to be accountable for what they do, there is in Africa a whole host of factors which affect the realities of political answerability. On occasions, individual politicians might be held responsible for events really outside their control, like drought or illness. More frequently, however, they can escape liability for policy decisions by resorting to the prevailing notions of external causality. In the world of the occult, responsibility for 'extra-ordinary' events is found within the bounds of the community. But in politics, it could be attributed to causes far and wide. And indeed, it is striking to see how systematically successful African politicians have been at explaining the problems of their country in terms of outside culprits: colonialism, imperialism, dependence, globalism, the World Bank, etc. Our argument is that such a causal approach to political accountability is possibly more than mere opportunism; it finds an echo in the collective cultural and religious consciousness of the general population.

Furthermore, this notion of causality has a direct bearing on political competition and links back with the difficulty of accepting a zero-sum-game political system. If it is the case that losing elections must have a cause (other than the one which is current in the West, namely, that one's party is not as popular as its competitors), then it is obvious that electoral defeat can have very serious consequences indeed. Is the failure an indication of some irredeemable flaw in religious character? Has a politician lost because of witchcraft, because he has neglected to pay proper homage to his ancestral spirits or because he has failed in some other way to meet his religious obligations? Have occult forces influenced the polls? Whatever the reason, it will be seen that electoral failure might not be readily accepted in Africa. Outside causes may well have to be found. The public humiliation of losing elections is thus much more instrumentally powerful than can possibly be accounted for in Western political theory. For this reason alone, multi-party electoral competition may have serious unintended effects and may even prove to be deeply destabilizing.

Practice

Whatever the political condition of Africa today, there is little doubt that religion is thriving. The facts cannot be denied: Africans are deeply religious; the realm of the irrational is growing, not diminishing; and religious beliefs or cults have become politically critical. This too is not unique to the continent. Islamic societies throughout the world show in which ways religion can influence the political order – and indeed Islam is active in African societies today. The question we pose here is whether there is an African 'way' of being religious which affects politics. Is there a relation between beliefs and culture which binds religion and politics in a manner that is specific to Africa?

The first part of a possible answer to that question is to consider the ways in which world religions have been Africanized. Is there a politically significant difference here between the African chapters of established religions (Catholic, Islamic and Protestant) and the so-called African churches, a profusion of which has been set up across the continent? It is customary, but probably a little simplistic, to see the former as associated with the elite and the latter with ordinary men and women. The extent to which that rule is confirmed or invalidated – differently in each country – is relevant to our understanding of the influence of religion on politics. So too is the degree to which both elites and populace share religious beliefs which are not easily accommodated in official, or even African, churches.

Another area to investigate is the relevance of religion and religious institutions to the relation between state and society. This ranges from the role of Islamic leaders in buttressing the existing one-party system, to the active role of national religious figures in the organization of the transition to multi-party democracy, or, finally, to the influence of African religious sects on the political complexion of local or even national government. Equally, one ought to study how 'traditional' African beliefs influence people's perceptions of the political realm: what, for example, are the obligations of a politician vis-à-vis a local spiritual leader? More generally, in which way is religion a factor for political change?

Given the above characteristics of African belief, we should like now to examine in greater detail the influence on African politics both of established religions and of witchcraft. We can do no more here than hint at the significance of religious practice on politics and we will concentrate on those aspects which are more immediately important to the understanding of the main contemporary political issues. We examine in turn the role of the church in society and politics; and the role of witchcraft in healing individuals, binding communities and acting as social leveller.[9]

(a) Church, power and society. There is here a well-established literature in African studies which we want neither to summarize nor to replicate. We shall only highlight those aspects of the formal and informal roles of churches which are both politically significant and which we feel have been neglected.

The first point to make concerns the distance between the established Christian and Islamic churches, on the one hand, and, on the

[9] For the purpose of our discussion church also includes here both Islamic institutions and the so-called African, or indigenous, churches.

other, the African or the newer (largely charismatic) Protestant sects. The former have both direct and indirect influence over the conduct of national politics. Their leaders belong to the country's top elite and as such have the power and authority to affect the world of politics. Although their role is usually unofficial, and relies essentially on the counsel they may offer the political professionals, they can in some circumstances take a more formal political role. Clearly, Muslim clerics can have a direct control on politics, as Islam does not recognize a formal boundary between the religious and the political.[10] More recently, however, leading Catholic and Protestant churchmen have also had central, if temporary, roles in the so-called democratic political transitions, most particularly perhaps as chairmen of national conferences or their equivalent.[11] Undoubtedly, the greater freedom of expression made possible by such developments has encouraged church leaders to speak out more forcefully on social and political issues.

The other role which established, particularly Christian, churches seek for themselves is that of speaking for society: acting as the voice of the voiceless. All churches would claim to reflect the concerns of their ordinary members and, to some extent, all have sought both to denounce political abuse and to demand that politicians become more accountable. But they too have suffered from the inadequate institutionalization of their churches. Church leaders have tried, with varying degree of success, to maintain their moral authority by keeping their distance from the politicians' deeds and, especially, misdeeds. Nevertheless, as part of the establishment, church leaders have not always managed to convince the population at large that the social and economic privileges which they not infrequently enjoy allow them the amount of political independence they claim.[12] Nor is it clear that established churches have succeeded in meeting the moral and practical needs of the ordinary people they purport to serve. Although few Africans formally abandon their church, they often turn to other religions capable of addressing their more immediate problems.

African churches and other more recently implanted religious sects, on the other hand, are closer to society, meaning here the local community, and usually have a more instrumentally practical role. Indeed, their very creation has usually been prompted by dissatisfaction with the established Christian or Islamic churches at their inability to meet the

---

[10] The experience of predominantly Muslim countries like Senegal illustrates the many direct and indirect ways in which the Islamic elites can influence the course of national politics.

[11] See an interesting new compilation on the role of religion, churches and clergymen in recent political transitions: Constantin and Coulon, 1997.

[12] See here the dossier on 'L'argent de Dieu' in *Politique Africaine*, 35 (October 1989).

most pressing needs of their congregations.[13] Clearly, as living conditions have worsened for the majority of Africans, there has been ample opportunity for new religious movements to focus attention on popular dissatisfaction. Clearly, too, newer sects have sought to reconcile the demands of the universalist Christian dogma with the religious beliefs of their converts. Those churches, like the Voodoo cult in Benin, which offer a path into the world of the occult (through exorcism, trance or communication with the dead) are likely to find an echo with ordinary people who worry about the effects of the irrational. Established churches are loath to go down that path, as is well illustrated by the fact that the Catholic Zambian prelate Mgr Milingo was hastily called to Rome for having sought to integrate 'African' healing practices into his ministry.[14]

It is not just that these more 'informal' churches address more directly the concerns of the majority of the population. It is also that they are often more congruent with prevailing beliefs in the irrational, or the occult. They are closer to the world in which ordinary people live. Some churches provide exorcism or healing while others offer hope that hard work and honesty will ultimately prevail. Many of the American sects engage their members directly, proposing very concrete steps to ameliorate one's life in exchange for a strong commitment to the church. There is thus a link between faith and the opportunity to improve one's condition. Some of these churches have shown themselves to be highly successful commercial enterprises, confirming thereby the reputation for self-improvement they have acquired. Above all, they offer relatively simple chains of causality, in which practical steps are outlined which hold the promise of tangible results, much in the ways that 'traditional' African beliefs do.

It would be naive, however, to think that religious belief in Africa is neatly compartmentalized. Membership of universalist and African churches is rarely mutually exclusive. Nor can affiliation to one particular church be taken as a commitment to the kind of religion that would leave no place for other, less 'orthodox', beliefs. The world of African religion is excessively catholic and allows room for an instrumental view of churches and other religious institutions. There may well be political reasons which dictate affiliation to one religion or another. It may be politically astute, or even merely expedient, for the elites, as well as for the populace, to become actively involved in one particular church. We know that in Brazzaville, for

---

[13] Although it is fair to say that Islam seems more capable both of adapting to local conditions and of fulfilling local needs than the established Christian churches. However, there are periodically reformist or fundamentalist Islamic movements, which have their roots in popular discontent.

[14] See Gerrie ter Haar, 1992.

example, there are now clear links between political rivals and competitor (universalist or African) churches.[15] The same is true almost everywhere in Africa. And while Muslims are, on the whole, more reluctant than Christians to dabble in sects, there are today many divisions within Islamic populations which also have directly instrumental causes, perhaps nowhere more clearly than in northern Nigeria where fundamentalists are now prepared to challenge the established religious order.

More important, however, is the question of the overlap between Christian or Muslim churches and the world of 'African' religious beliefs. It has been argued that Islam was often more successful in Africa than Christianity because it was both more open to the local world of the irrational and more pragmatic in its acceptance of local practices (of which polygamy is the most notorious). There is much truth in this view, although Islamic scholars would reject the overall argument that African Islam is a syncretic religion. Be that as it may, the success of Islam in Africa may well be due, in part at least, to the extent to which it is perceived to be more accommodating of local religious beliefs than universalist Christian churches. Neither, however, would accept a direct link with the world of the occult. And yet there is ample evidence that witchcraft remains central today to the lives of most Africans, including Christians and Muslims.

(b) Witchcraft, society and politics. Our concern here is not to explore the whole question of witchcraft *per se*, on which there is a profusion of (chiefly anthropological) material, but merely to suggest some of the ways in which it is relevant both to the notion of power and to the practice of modern politics. Indeed, what is interesting about witchcraft today is the extent to which it has managed to modernize, to respond to the demands of the contemporary world and to adapt to the needs of Africans in the post-colonial societies in which they live. To give one example, Peter Geschiere has shown, in a recent article about the current importance of witchcraft in modern Cameroonian politics, how the realm of the irrational had a bearing on the link between city elites and their village of origin.[16] There are, of course, many reasons why this is so – the assumption that witchcraft would disappear with modernity was always dubious – but we wish to look more closely at three important aspects of witchcraft.

The first has to do with healing. It is often overlooked by political analysts that one of the primary concerns of witchcraft has to do with

---

[15] See Joseph Tonda, 'De l'exorcisme comme mode de démocratisation', in Constantin & Coulon, *op. cit.*
[16] Peter Geschiere, 1996.

what we in the West would call therapy. Although much work focuses on the more 'medical' aspects of this healing process, witchcraft has also been instrumental in providing 'treatment' for psychological or social disorders associated with the modern post-colonial world. These ills, it is true, usually manifest themselves in tensions within the family, but they are in fact often the result of problems in society at large: poverty, unemployment, violence, alienation, etc. In any event, these are ailments for which there are no ready medical or psychological treatments. Given the present situation in most African countries, it is clear why there is an ever increasing demand for religious beliefs to have instrumentally concrete results.

For this reason alone, belief in witchcraft is unlikely to diminish, particularly in urban settings where such problems are more widespread and more acute than in rural areas. Witchcraft can be said to contribute to the maintenance of the cohesion of society, in so far as it helps resolve problems which might otherwise result in even higher social discontent and strife. There is a price to pay, however, in that such healing relies on finding a (real rather than imaginary) culprit. While that guilt is usually located within the family circle, this is not always the case, particularly in the cities. Furthermore, the search for the felon, unless s(he) readily agrees to expiate for the guilt, can have socially destabilizing effects. Hence, there are periodic attacks by African governments on the presumed practitioners of sorcery.[17]

Witchcraft, with its focus on the family and kinship, is also instrumental in binding communities together, since it seeks to find resolution to problems which might otherwise divide people and tear at the communal fabric. Given what we know of the nature of the relation between the individual and the community, this instrumental effect is bound to be politically consequential. The rigours of such religious beliefs will of necessity influence the behaviour of politicians. As we have seen, the very legitimacy of their representativeness is tied to local demands, and the continued success of politicians will very likely require that they propitiate such religious beliefs. It is clear, for example, that national political figures, however powerful, remain vulnerable to accusations of witchcraft made in their home region. And in an age of party political competition, it can readily be imagined how politically effective such charges of 'anti-communal' behaviour might be. This is indeed one of the ways in which multi-party electoral systems could seriously increase the role of witchcraft in modern African societies.

The point about this aspect of kinship is that it provides one means of enforcing local accountability on those who seek political support.

---

[17] See here Peter Geschiere, 1995, particularly Chapter 5 on the trials held in Cameroon of 'sorcerers'.

Witchcraft may, of course, not be what Western political theorists had in mind when they conceptualized the democratic political system as one in which there were interlocking checks and balances, but it is clearly a working reality of African politics. Although in most cases local communities will rejoice in seeing one of their own occupy high office, a charge of witchcraft can easily be used as the ultimate sanction against those politicians who fail to live up to local expectations. No matter how prominent and powerful a national political figure, there is no escaping the political impact which such a sanction can have. And a politician without local support cannot survive for long, even at the national level.

The same might be said for the third instrumental aspect of witch-craft: its role as a social leveller. It has often been noted that accusations of witchcraft are made against those who have enriched themselves. It is, of course, possible to dismiss such charges as jealousy on the part of those members of the community who have not been so economically successful. But this would be to ignore the commonly held view that Africans do not, on the whole, suffer from puritanical zeal or self-deny-ing guilt. On the contrary, wealth is much to be admired, even if it does generate some envy. This explains, as we have seen, why riches have to be displayed as ostentatiously as resources will allow. Generally, then, members of a community will praise the wealth of its economi-cally successful kin as much as their political might, since such success is certain to rebound on them favourably.

One of the reasons, however, for such rejoicing is that the wealthy are expected to share their wealth with their community. Affluence imposes rules of generosity which are implemented through patronage. There is an inbuilt bias within African social theory in favour of the redistribu-tion of the wealth accumulated by the successful individuals to their constituent communities. This bias can easily be perceived by success-ful and Westernized individuals as an intolerable constraint on the use of the fruits of their labour and as an impediment to further economic expansion. How can they develop their business if they are expected to redistribute the bulk of their profits? It is bad enough to have responsi-bility for the extended family; obligations to one's community can be perceived as being excessive.

The tension between the elites and the rural communities from which they hail is fertile ground for witchcraft. Here it can be seen that witchcraft can act as a force for preventing excessive economic differ-entials and for encouraging redistribution within communities in two distinct ways. The first is that it puts pressure on the wealthy to dis-burse much of their profits in their home region either directly through existing networks of patronage or indirectly through ostenta-tion and by investing locally. The second is that a successful negotiation of the community's acceptance of one's economic prosperity brings not only communal benefits but enables the wealthy to acquire the legitimate trappings of rank and prestige. For example, in the Bamiléké region of Cameroon the contribution by wealthy businessmen towards the rebuilding of 'traditional' chieftaincies after the UPC insurrection enabled those successful entrepreneurs to 'purchase' positions of prestige within their home communities.[18] From this perspective, witchcraft appears less a throwback to outdated traditions than a mechanism of social regulation which brings both material benefit and communal cohesion to the locality.

The question which is often asked is whether witchcraft is an impediment to political modernization. If we assume that modernization is synonymous with Westernization, then it probably is. But if we mean whether it might contribute to finding new modes of plausible political accountability in contemporary Africa, then the answer is more complex. Like ethnicity in this respect, witchcraft is one of the few means of 'indigenous' social responsibility available, however crude its practice may be in reality. Far be it from us to advocate the use of witchcraft for political purposes. We want only to ask whether it might not be important to take into account the constantly evolving effects of the irrational upon contemporary political practices in Africa.

One further question which merits investigation is whether the present transitions to multi-party political systems are not likely to result in the greater importance of the world of the irrational. Indeed, as political competition intensifies, witchcraft and religion may become more, rather than less, salient. There is certainly evidence that they have both found ways of adapting to the demands of modernity.

[18] Geschiere, 1995.

6

**Crime
& Enrichment**

The Profits of
Violence

There is undeniably in Africa today a high level of violence[1] – not just
in situations where law and order have broken down entirely but also
where conditions are deemed to be relatively stable. Indeed, there are
now very few countries on the continent where brutality does not
encroach directly on the daily lives of ordinary Africans as they go
about their business. Or rather, the business of living and working,
especially in the cities (and Africa continues to urbanize at a frightening pace), is increasingly fraught with the danger of suffering violence
and crime.

If violence is defined as the arbitrary use – or threat of the use – of
physical force in order to achieve compliance, then it is obvious that
most Africans are regularly suffering from it. This ranges from thieving, harassment and thuggery to extortion, police malpractice, armed
robbery, murder and war. Since in most African countries the 'state'
not only fails to protect the population from crime but is itself responsible for a high level of violence, both through the direct abuse of
power and because of its predatory nature, it is not surprising that
ordinary men and women will seek to devise alternate strategies for
coping with arbitrary force. As is the case in all disordered and poorly
regulated societies, where crime is endemic, the very management of
violence turns into a resource for some.

Organized violence thrives in poor societies where politics is weakly
institutionalized, where law and order is fragile and where the parallel
economy is strong, all of which are features of the African patrimonial
system. The point of organized violence is to regulate that part of society which can usefully be marshalled for the pursuit of well-defined

---

[1] We use here the notion of violence to include crime, as most crime in Africa contains an explicit or implicit resort to violence.

economic aims. And in a situation where the government has become so weak economically, the resources of parallel informal organizations (some with worldwide connections) are growing daily in importance.

There is, of course, a wide range of different experiences in Africa, but it can safely be said that violence, in its most diverse forms (from the physical to the psychological), is the ever present backdrop of the present social 'order'. Our concern here is to understand how such violence, and the need to be protected from it, are instrumentalized and what effects this may have on the politics of contemporary Africa. We shall concentrate in the first part on the violence of ordinary life, ranging from thieving and petty crime to internal war. In the second part, we shall discuss the international dimensions of what has been dubbed the increasing 'criminalization' of the continent.

The violence of everyday life: from petty crime to civil war

Everyday violence in Africa essentially takes two forms: thuggery or crime, and 'state' violence. Coping with them requires strategies of survival and counter-measures, which in turn demand the protection of organized networks. Thuggery and crime are resented everywhere in the world but in Africa the authorities provide little shield against them. Africans thus seek protection from crime where they are able to get it, even if this involves meeting violence with violence.[2] Crime and counter-criminal measures can in this way easily induce a spiral of greater violence in society. The same is true of the abuse by the police and armed forces, both of which are notorious in Africa for preying on the local population. People seek protection from official exaction which, quite rightly, they most often perceive as eminently arbitrary.

If we are to understand how crime is instrumentalized, however, we need to examine in greater detail the networks which seek to organize and make productive the high level of violence found in African societies. We must, in other words, investigate what might be called its 'moral' economy.[3] A primary level of analysis would distinguish between two types of networks: one legal and visible, if informal; the other illegal and more clandestine. The first would typically be in the hands of what we might be tempted to call 'patrons'; the second those whom we might see as 'bosses'. But such a dichotomy between, effectively, the licit and the illicit implies a (chiefly Eurocentric) normative

[2] Hence the tendency for local people to mete immediate justice when they can or to organize vigilante groups.

[3] As we do in our discussion of corruption in Chapter 7.

analysis which is largely irrelevant to Africa. Irrelevant not because there are no well-accepted notions of the legal and illegal but because, as we would expect, the activities of the networks run by patrons and bosses resemble and straddle each other considerably.

A more profitable conceptual distinction consists in looking at the range of activities organized by these networks, legal or illegal, from the perspective of legitimacy and accountability. The key question here is how criminal activities can serve the patrimonial purposes of patron–client relationships. In Africa, the realm of clientelism and the world of crime overlap. The means to patrimonialism, including at times violence, are legitimate insofar as patrons are perceived to discharge their obligations to clients. This is another way of saying that, within a patrimonial social system, accountability takes the form of redistribution. Where patrons nourish their clientelistic networks, the manner in which they have managed to obtain their resources will very largely be taken to be legitimate, even if it is illicit.

It is for this reason that it is analytically dubious to speak of the 'criminalization of the state in Africa'[4] outside the context of what is perceived to be legitimate by the beneficiaries of the so-called criminal activities. As with mafia-type operations throughout the world, the loss of legitimacy derives not from the illegal nature of some activities but from the dissolution of accountability. It is when patrons cease to redistribute their legal or ill-gotten gains to their clients – that is, in effect, to be accountable to them – that their activities become criminal, in the sense of being perceived as illegitimate by those who might have stood to benefit but no longer do. For us, therefore, the notion of criminal should only be used to refer to an illicit activity which is also clearly illegitimate in the eyes of those concerned.

There has always existed in Africa a wide range of activities (such as corruption) which, although illicit from a strictly constitutional or legal point of view, have been regarded as patrimonially legitimate by the bulk of the population. In the present context of severe economic crisis, where patrons are short of resources, there is evidently an extension of illicit and criminal activities – with the inevitable corollary of greater violence. How legitimate such activities are deemed by the population at large to be is, in our view, an eminently practical question, and not an *a priori* value judgement.

That is why we need to re-examine the role of patrons in Africa's heightened climate of violence and crime. Patrons work in the open, legitimately, even if what they do has extensive subterranean roots. They need to be seen. Their role consists in using all available

---

[4] As does Bayart in Bayart, Ellis and Hibou, 1998. Chabal's review of the French edition of the book appears in *Politique Africaine*, 67 (October 1997).

resources to fashion instrumentally useful links between the centres of power and society. Thus, they operate simultaneously in the world of politics and of the economy. They may be politicians or businessmen but what makes them patrons is their ability to provide their clients with ways of profiting from the activities of their networks while at the same time being protected from violence. Typically, they will ensure that their clients are not harassed by the police or the armed forces and that they can go about their business without fear of rival networks or criminals. Such protection requires both the ability to deter violence and to meet force with force when necessary.

(a) The business of violence. Politicians are often effective patrons because they may have influence over the ways in which officialdom affects their clients. Nevertheless, in many African societies business-men, entrepreneurs or traders are more powerful simply because their economic means are more substantial and less prone to the vagaries of politics. In practice, however, the difference between the two is more symbolic than real, since the overlap of the world of politics and that of business is one of the most salient features of contemporary Africa. What brings both sides together is the determination to control and contain disorder within manageable, that is instrumentally produc-tive, boundaries. What patrons do not want is for violence to get out of control.

In effect, patrons are thus 'licensees' of violence in that they possess that attribute – the exercise of coercion – which in more politically institutionalized societies is the strict preserve of the state. Control of and protection from violence, or coercion, are thus unofficially devolved. Patrons can access or restrain official force, most notably in military regimes, while at the same time maintaining their own corps of armed men to protect clients and counter the violence of competi-tive networks. Their power is in this way both overt, since they can count on the local police or military commander; and covert, since they can unleash unseen militias to enforce compliance. The unedify-ing story of violence in the Congo, which culminated in 1997 with the expulsion of the sitting president (Pascal Lissouba) by the former pres-ident (Denis Sassou Nguesso), is an emblematic case of the relation-ship between central power and 'private' violence.

Patrons are key players in what is called the informal sector, where success depends on the ease with which economic transactions can evade official control or hindrance. The whole of the parallel economy of African countries rests on the operation of vast national, regional and even international networks, the functioning of which demands both protection from violence and access to the threat of coercion against competitors. Patrons attempt to regulate the use of force as smoothly and economically as is possible. Smuggling, for example, calls for the ability to buy off those officials who might be in a position to impede the illicit trade as well as the means to call on armed protection if needed. Similarly, the transit of drugs from South America and Asia through Africa to Europe requires effective protection of the complex networks involved.

Practically, then, patrons are those who can both influence the arbitrariness of official coercion and control private violence to ensure the functioning of the productive networks linking the informal worlds of economy and politics. What, it may be asked, is the distinction between the informal and the criminal, in a context in which patrons are also involved in clearly illegal activities? The difference is plain, even if it is not easily understood by those who view Africa solely from a Western perspective. There are in African societies well-understood, if not always well-defined, rules of conduct which mark clear boundaries between the informal sector and the criminal world. The informal may be illicit but it is legitimate because it rests on a principle of common clientelistic accountability. The criminal is illegitimate because it is unaccountable and based only on duress.

Criminality thrives in disordered societies such as Africa's simply because it can operate easily in the interstices of the existing networks which delineate the competitive boundaries between 'official' activities and those of the parallel sector. The overlap between formal and informal as well as the intense rivalry between patrons create an ideal framework for the spread of criminal activities. This criminal world is diverse – from small-scale racketeering to wholesale pillage – but what makes it particularly effective in Africa is the frightening ease with which it can use violence. Devoid of police protection, people will thus either turn to patrons for succour or, inevitably and reluctantly, they will seek help from the bosses of other local criminal gangs.

In this world of disorder and in the face of such a bewildering array of possible sources of violence, Africans will understandably fall back on the most familiar resources. These are overwhelmingly those associated with security and protection: that is, the communal and the religious. Thus, the search for protection against violence or the attempt to devise counter-measures will often be channelled through 'tribalism' or witchcraft. Indeed, in a situation where uncertainty and arbitrariness prevail, where life outside violence is virtually impossible, the use of identity or the irrational as a weapon for survival, or counter-attack, makes eminent sense. The violence of ordinary life, therefore, becomes a powerful force for the 're-traditionalization' of society.

(b) The makers of war. Above and beyond the conditions of violence discussed above, which characterize most African societies, there has been in the last ten years an increase in the number and viciousness of civil conflicts. From the wars in Sudan, Rwanda, Burundi, Angola and Mozambique, which go back several decades, to those of Liberia, Sierra Leone, Congo and Zaire, which have flared more recently, there is now a large part of Africa living in the shadow of armed strife. What we want to discuss here is not just the genesis of such conflicts, which is obviously to be found in the poor sedimentation of the post-colonial political order, but more particularly the brutal expressions which many of them have taken.

If the attempted genocide in Rwanda is the most notorious example of such savageness, there is unfortunately a large number of other cases, from Mozambique to Sierra Leone, of extremely brutal and cruel civil violence. Is the occurrence of internal conflicts which exhibit such brutality a result of the general increase of violence in African society? Or is it part of a more sinister new development in which modern civil violence is becoming ritualized in a new form of 'barbarity'? What can the logic be of conflicts in which there is widespread destruction of the social and economic fabric of the country? Why is it thought necessary to indulge in acts of degrading brutishness such as the mutilation of civilians?

Finally, there are a growing number of cases where civil order comes to rest in the hands of warlords. The phenomenon of warlordism is, of course, not new and there is much to learn from those non-African societies where it has thrived. Here we need to understand whether today's modernizing Africa has given rise to a certain number of specific features which make warlordism a viable option. The issue is not so much to explain individual examples of warlordism but to explore how such a phenomenon may have become one way in which disorder is instrumentalized in contemporary Africa.

The first point to make about civil conflicts is that they are part of the present-day calculus of power in contemporary Africa. As the violence of everyday life grows and the institutional mechanisms for regulating society increasingly fail, the pressures for social strife intensify. In a situation of economic crisis (absence of development) and sharpening poverty, the resources of patrons diminish and their ability to control disorder decreases. Bosses become more prominent, criminal activity prospers and the devolution of violence moves apace. Force becomes the major currency of social and political transactions.

The shift from civil disorder to civil war, however, marks a qualitative leap in the escalation of violence which is usually triggered by events beyond the immediate control of the masters of domestic coercion. It may be, as in Angola and Mozambique, that the regime is facing regional or even international opposition and must thus endure a domestic enemy long supplied from outside. It may be, as in Somalia, that the social basis of the existing political order is suddenly fractured by a combination of internal and external pressures. It may be, as in

Ethiopia and Zaire, that civil disorder results in the breakdown of the national political structure. It may be, finally, as in Liberia or Sierra Leone, that the failures of the patrimonial political system and the ambitions of frustrated politicians degenerate into full-scale civil war.

Whatever the reasons for the breakdown of civil order, there is no denying the extreme escalation in violence which most of these conflicts unleash. Where resources are available, as in Ethiopia and Angola, they can turn into full-scale conventional warfare, including air combat. Where the fighting factions cannot afford sophisticated weaponry, as in Mozambique or Sierra Leone, violence easily degenerates into brutalizing terror, plumbing the depths of depravity (such as using children as soldiers or torturing and mutilating civilians). Although it is easy to interpret such paroxysms of violence as the evidence of atavistic characteristics of the continent, there are good instrumental reasons for what is happening.

There are essentially two types of armed conflicts in contemporary Africa: the political and the criminal. They are in effect nothing but the continuation by other means of the violence of everyday life. Although, as we have already made clear, there is considerable overlap between the two, the conceptual distinction between them is clear. Political conflicts, however brutal, are relatively straightforward struggles for power which are considered legitimate by a significant proportion of the populations that support the warring parties. Criminal conflicts, however justified they are claimed to be by their leaders, are not considered politically legitimate by those who are engulfed in them, precisely because it is well understood that such violence is but the outcome of the private greed of the war-makers.

The notion of political conflict does not imply that people find violence desirable or even acceptable, but simply that they concede its inevitability on political grounds which are congruent with (at least some of) their beliefs and aspirations. In Angola, Ethiopia, Mozambique and Zaire, civil war was seen by many (though by no means all) as the last resort for necessary political change. Enough civilians accepted, however reluctantly, that violence was the only means to reform a political order with which they were dissatisfied. That is why Kabila's assault on the central 'state' was viewed as legitimate by so many Zairians. Of course, a political conflict can become criminal if its legitimacy dissolves. It is clear, for example, that the present continuation of civil strife in Angola is now rejected by all Angolans, except for those on both sides who have become entrepreneurs of war. It is today very largely a criminal conflict, aided and abetted by foreign economic interests.

Conversely, the notion of criminal civil conflict does not imply that some sections of the population, chiefly the disaffected youth who benefit, do not find instrumental use (rather than legitimacy) in the violence in which they are involved. What it does mean is that the opposing sides have no substantial support based on a conception of what the political ambitions of the protagonists might be. It means too, and this is most significant, that all civilians are at risk of suffering violence from any side in the conflict. Force here becomes most narrowly instrumental and is used, as required, to ensure immediate compliance regardless of the social or political consequences. At its most extreme, as in Sierra Leone, such violence violates most of the commonly held social, communal or religious boundaries.

There would seem to be two exceptions to the above: one is ethnic war, of which the most extreme is the Rwandan case, and the other is warlordism, of which Somalia appears most paradigmatic. Singular as these conflicts are, and we explain below why, we would argue that they do not in fact invalidate our general analysis of civil violence in Africa. We discuss them in turn.

Although the events in Rwanda and Burundi which culminated in the attempted genocide of the Tutsis in Rwanda in 1994 are particularly gruesome in their ethnic logic, they have well-defined historical roots. They are political conflicts which have become fanatically criminalized, as have other similar conflicts elsewhere, most recently in the former Yugoslavia. What this means is that the economic, social and political causes of discontent in Rwanda and Burundi, that go back to dynamics engendered already in the pre-colonial period and were considerably aggravated under colonial rule, were channelled by extremist politicians into a genocidal frenzy, which is nothing other than the most systematically criminal form of civil violence available to the makers of war.

In other words, legitimate popular grievances and dissatisfaction with the existing social, economic and political order were used as pretexts by politicians bent on asserting themselves by means of criminal terror. Such extreme violence, however, does not command legitimacy outside the narrowest circle of politicians, because in the present circumstances of Rwanda and Burundi it only serves to unleash massive, and potentially counter-genocidal, violence. Very few Hutus in Rwanda seriously believe that they can actually resolve their problems by eliminating all Tutsis, if only because there are no such things as entirely pure Hutus and Tutsis. In the end, therefore, civil strife in Rwanda and Burundi does not derive from a peculiarly African 'tendency' to indulge in ethnic war but results, more prosaically, from the same causes as afflict other similar societies, in Africa or elsewhere.

The case of Somalia is, on the face of it, quite different, as civil violence there appears entirely to be channelled along the lines of warlordism. Indeed, Somalia exhibits what might be termed the most purely classical characteristics in Africa of warlord politics: that is, clan-based instrumentalized violence. Although the events in Somalia seem to have baffled the international community, they are not entirely mysterious. When the dividends of a secular nationalist and Marxist dictatorship based on a coalition of clan support began to dissipate, the political order of clientelism and repression collapsed. Armed insurrection had begun in 1982 but it was in 1988, following the defeat of the opposition Somali National Movement (SNM), that clan-based violence intensified. In the absence of any political consensus within the opposition, the challenge to Siad Barre, which succeeded in ousting him in 1991, heightened clan rivalry and, ultimately, degenerated into criminal violence, where elsewhere in Black Africa it might have resulted in ethnic strife.[5]

The logic of warlord violence in Somalia is, again unsurprisingly, both political and criminal. There is, on the one hand, the attempt by some warlords to impose a new political order by force, order which can only be restored by negotiations – as has happened following the secession in the North. There is, on the other, the purely instrumental use by certain warlords of clan-based violence for criminal ends, as is most obviously the case in current disputes within Mogadishu and some of the other southern cities. What distinguishes warlordism in Somalia from that found in other parts of Africa, therefore, is its structured social and political clan foundations, rather than its criminal tendencies.

In much of the rest of Africa, warlordism is defined in more narrowly functional terms: warlords are, quite literally, businessmen of war, that is, they wield violence as the main instrument of their economic activity. In societies devoid of major economic resources, or where agriculture predominates, they use violence to survive and feed their clientelistic networks. Much of Renamo's activities during the civil war in Mozambique conformed to this pattern. In areas rich in mineral resources – as in Sierra Leone – they can set up extensive business operations, with wide international ramifications. Clearly, and whatever else it may be, the war in Angola is very largely one in which Savimbi operates as a consummate entrepreneur of war with access to diamonds, even if he has national ambitions going beyond those of a mere warlord.

There is, however, one distinct form of civil violence which ostensibly escapes easy classification: the religious. There are today in Africa a range of religiously based movements that use violence to further their ends. At one extreme, we find, as in Nigeria, Muslim

---

[5] See here Alex de Waal, 'Contemporary Warfare in Africa', in Mary Kaldor and Basker Vashee (eds), *New Wars* (London: Pinter, 1998).

fundamentalist groups with a clearly defined political agenda. Their action is relatively easy to understand in that, for all the local African considerations, they resemble other similar movements elsewhere in the Muslim world, from Algeria to Malaysia. At the other extreme are organizations such as the Lords Resistance Army (LRA) in Uganda, with a millenarian social and political objective grounded in an Africanized form of Christian belief. Such movements are clearly political in the broad sense of reflecting a (relatively restricted) moral position on society but their millenarian agenda places them firmly outside the political and criminal organizations we have discussed so far.

We turn now to the thorny issue of the increasingly brutal forms which civil violence has assumed in Africa, for instance in Mozambique, Liberia and Sierra Leone. The question for us is: how can such seemingly mindless cruelty serve any meaningful instrumental purpose? Indeed, the nature of violence in these conflicts confounds our analysis in that they appear to exhibit quite clear pathological characteristics which are not consistent with the use of force as a means of gaining power. If brutality is visited arbitrarily on those who might have constituted the movement's natural constituency, then it becomes difficult to see how it serves the political aims of the leadership. How can any movement justify cutting off limbs or forcing children to kill their parents and siblings?

There is, of course, no simple answer to this question but a study of the use of terror by Renamo in Mozambique and the Revolutionary United Front (RUF) in Sierra Leone might help to shed some light. In Mozambique, it is in retrospect clear that Renamo's violence was instrumental in that it enabled the movement to achieve its three main aims: to destroy the state's infrastructure; to discredit Frelimo policies particularly in the countryside; and to nourish the client base that would enable it to survive and develop as opposition.[6] In retrospect too, it seems clear that, following the peace accord, Renamo was not overpenalized by the electorate, receiving as it did over a third of the votes.

In Sierra Leone, the picture is more murky since the conflict is far from over. But as Paul Richards has argued in his recent book, there is an instrumental, if perversely obscene, logic to the RUF's deeds which is not unlike that of Renamo's.[7] The RUF does provide an ideological underpinning to its terror and it does have specific political aims which are susceptible to negotiation. Understanding the logic which makes sense of the RUF's unspeakable violence, however, requires an

---

[6] See Christian Geffray, *La cause des armes au Mozambique: anthropologie d'une guerre civile* (Paris: Karthala, 1990).
[7] Richards, 1996.

analysis of the irrational (as discussed in Chapter 5). And it is the great merit of Richards's (1998) article to offer an explanation (though not a justification) of the deep historical, psychological and religious roots of the civil conflict in Sierra Leone. He writes:[8]

> My argument is that the RUF became a secular sect, that its sectarian tendencies originate in a preoccupation with social exclusion and educational privilege, and the bizarre patterns of violence associated with its forest incarceration are a response, shaped by sectarian values, to a *revival* of patrimonial forces ranged against it.

Richards's (1996) book also provides us with a cogently argued and conceptually well-informed case study of the ways in which the apparent violent re-traditionalization of Africa is in fact an indication of its pangs of modernization. His argument, which is probably valid anywhere in Africa albeit in a locally specific variant, is that the conflict in Sierra Leone is the product of the country's difficult transition to modernity. The actors involved in the violence reason in terms of modernity – social, cultural, economic and political – but the instruments they employ are steeped in the culture and history of their people. To the young in particular, the war is about modern issues of life, work and identity. Their resort to seemingly 'barbaric' violence, often modelled on Rambo, is in fact merely a singularly distorted vision of what force can achieve in the world in which they live. Here too, it can be seen that armed violence all too easily leads to an instrumentally plausible re-traditionalization of society.

Violence and crime: the international dimension

Although it is often argued that Africa is now marginalized within the world economy, there is a very strong international dimension to the continent's profits from crime. Indeed, the thesis about the 'criminalization' of the African state turns on the importance of Africa within a growing number of international mafia-type networks. From this perspective, Africa's economy is now becoming increasingly active in the informal trade in illegal substances (from drugs to toxic waste) and a vast array of other smuggling operations, as well as an area of choice for money laundering. The argument, then, is that Africa's economy is very largely tied up with its involvement in illegal or criminal activities, to which the patrimonial nature of politics and the generalized level of violence in society are ideally suited. We discuss briefly both

[8] Richards, 1998: 79.

the international dimension of violence in Africa and the continent's involvement in international illicit activities.

One of the striking features of Africa today is the extent to which violence crosses borders. It is not just the millions of refugees who flee strife in their own countries and in the process contribute to the destabilization of the societies in which they settle, as in the Sudan and the Horn of Africa or in the Great Lakes and the surrounding Central African countries. It is also the extent to which armed opposition to regimes in place operates, overtly or covertly, from neighbouring countries, as in the civil conflicts of Angola, Mozambique, Zaire, Chad or Sierra Leone. Conversely, attempts to reduce civil conflict are becoming more international, albeit under the guise of African intervention forces, as in Liberia or Sierra Leone. Finally, there are the myriad ways in which conflict in one country spills over into others, as in Rwanda, Zaire, Burundi or Liberia.

It is also, and less spectacularly, the insidious process of violence against particular ethnic or professional groups which has clear international ramifications. Indeed, as economic and social problems become more acute, there is a strong tendency in many African countries to find foreign, or allegedly foreign, scapegoats. Mauritanians are attacked in Dakar and expelled from Senegal, prompting retaliation from Mauritania. 'Illegal' workers in Nigeria or Côte d'Ivoire are returned forcibly to their country of origin. Tuaregs in Niger are forced to flee persecution from their own government. Somalis are thrown out of Kenya. Zairian Tutsis are evicted from their land.

This growing internationalization of domestic violence becomes instrumentalized in different criminal ways. The movement of vast numbers across borders provides boundless opportunities to expand and consolidate networks throughout the continent. Perhaps the most spectacular example here is South Africa which, in a matter of the few years since travel restrictions have been lifted, has become by far the largest transit area for the most notable criminal activities, from drugs to illegal weapons. In this respect, at least, South Africa has rapidly become 'colonized' by the rest of Black Africa. There are now throughout the continent covert networks which operate more smoothly and efficiently than most governments and strengthen thereby the links between formal and informal politics.

There is, furthermore, another disturbing aspect to the management of violence in Africa, which might be called the devolution of state coercion to private foreign concerns. Faced with increasing violence, or civil conflict, within their own countries, and unable either to maintain or to trust their own armed forces and police, African governments with the means to do so now 'buy in' internal security. Here, the paradigmatic example is the South African-based company, Executive

Outcomes (EO), itself the result of the privatization of the former South African counter-insurgency personnel and expertise. EO's greatest successes have been in Angola and Sierra Leone, where insurgent activity had jeopardized diamond production: two countries, therefore, with the resources to pay for private security.

Although EO claims that it only works 'legally' for *bona fide* governments, such 'buying in' of private conflict resolution forces from outside has ominous implications. In particular, it lends itself to a process whereby some African governments will become even less accountable to the people over whom they rule and even more involved with outside commercial agents, of whom few doubt that they dabble in illegal or criminal activities. Similarly, the involvement of African peacekeeping forces, in countries like Liberia and Sierra Leone, has led to claims that some foreign contingents, such as the Nigerian, have facilitated the internationalization of illicit trade or criminal activities.

Two other aspects of the international ramifications of the activities of African commercial networks shed additional light on the instrumentalization of crime: drug trafficking and covert financial activities. The first is well understood now and is best illustrated by the emergence of a powerful Nigerian complex of networks which have made a strong impact in the United States. It is claimed by the US anti-drug establishment that the Nigerians have now become the single largest supplier of cocaine and heroin.[9] The reason for such spectacular success is supposed to be their ability to control both ends of the market, from producers in South-east Asia or Latin America to distributors in American cities. Here, it would appear that the African 'genius' for trade is finding its fullest expression.

The point here is not so much to verify whether the Nigerian presence in North America is as strong as it is rumoured to be, but to understand what consequences for African societies such illicit commerce may have. First, the enormous resources generated by the trade strengthen the informal economies of these countries. Second, this business inevitably bolsters the role of patrons and leads to an increasing overlap between the legal and the illicit. Third, the involvement of officials and politicians in drug trafficking, which is scarcely to be denied, amplifies further the informalization of politics, as discussed in Part I of this book. Fourth, the internationalization of the financial base of local politics is beneficial to clientelism but is inimical to the

---

[9] See Observatoire Géopolitique des Drogues, *Etat des drogues; drogue des Etats* (Paris: Hachette, 1994) and United States Department of State, Bureau for International Narcotics and Law Enforcement Affairs, *International Narcotics Control Strategy Report*, Washington, DC, April 1995.

country's development, at least in the way it is normally understood in the West.[10]

Covert financial activities, in which Africa essentially serves as an international centre for the laundering of illicit money, is yet another area where the continent is showing itself adept at the instrumentalization of crime. Although most of these activities are by definition difficult to bring to light, we have in the history of the involvement of the Bank of Commerce and Credit International (better known as BCCI) in Africa a well-documented case study which makes the point in ample detail.[11] It now seems clear that the BCCI was the most successful banking institution ever to straddle the world of legitimate and illicit financial activities and as such found fertile ground in Africa. Indeed, within a few years the BCCI established itself as the major foreign bank on the continent, with decisive access to governments in a large number of African countries.

The operations of the BCCI in Africa are complex but they can be summarized as follows. The bank would seek influence among the African political and economic elites by providing personal (financial, business, commercial and other) services. Once it had established its credentials, it used Africa to launder money from illicit activities throughout the world. In exchange, the BCCI would, for example, facilitate the transfer of foreign currency out of the country, help in falsifying import/export transactions, cover illicit financial deals, or lend money despite the absence of the required guarantees of creditworthiness. Most importantly, perhaps, it would help temporarily to swell a country's financial reserves in order to lend credibility to its case that it was meeting the budgetary conditions required by international financial institutions (typically the IMF). The BCCI is now defunct but it would be naive to think that Africans have not found elsewhere the financial partners they need. Nor would it be unreasonable to suppose that other banks are willing to provide at least some of the financial 'services' which the BCCI so willingly offered – after all, drug money was successfully laundered long before the BCCI was created

The important point to make here is that African entrepreneurs are closely connected to an informal world economy which serves their purposes well. The instrumentalization of violence and crime at the local level readily finds the international channels which make possible the trade on which wealth is built. Such enrichment, most of which is unrecorded, serves to nourish the domestic networks that

---

[10] See here our discussion of development in Chapter 9.
[11] L. Gurwin and P. Truell, *False Profits: the inside story of BCCI, the world's most corrupt financial empire* (Boston: Houghton Mifflin & Co, 1992).

make possible the functioning of patronage and provide the resources to ensure the efficient operation of the 'parallel', that is, the real, economy.

To conclude, the disorderly state of the formal political and economic structures and the high level of violence in most countries in Africa are used as resources by the 'businessmen' of crime. These assorted patrons and warlords are the only ones able both to provide some order and to facilitate the productive domestication of prevailing disorder. Given how porous the 'state' is, the current pressures to liberalize the economy and introduce multi-party electoral systems are likely to conspire to allow even greater scope for the 'privatization' of the illicit, a process which further reinforces the power of this shadowy entrepreneurial elite.

III

The Productivity of Economic 'Failure'

The third part of the book examines the political complexion of Africa's economic predicament. The aim here is not to rehearse the nature of the economic crisis or to adduce yet more evidence of the continent's failure to develop, but to focus attention on the ways in which individuals, communities and societies adapt to a situation in which development (as it is normally understood in the West) has not taken place. The question as to why contemporary Africa is in such a parlous economic state is complex, dependent as it is on a combination of external and internal factors which it is important to identify. Here, however, we shall be as concerned with the historical reasons for the existing situation as with the actual operation of Africa's economies in their present context.

We shall want to investigate the extent to which our current perception of Africa's crisis – based on standard development theory – is preventing us from analysing the ways in which the continent's economies do work. In particular, we shall enquire whether the vitality of the informal sector and the exploitation of the resources engendered by disorder do not in fact amount to more substantial marketable activities than is usually understood. We shall thus focus attention on how Africans manage in the circumstances which they face, through an examination of three specific areas of enquiry: corruption, dependence and development.

Corruption in Africa is at once the most familiar and the least understood of issues. It is familiar because, however it is defined, it is clearly endemic. It is poorly understood because we lack the investigative tools to make sense of its rationality. Explanations range from the ethical to the futile, seeing it, at one extreme, as a dereliction of given societal norms of behaviour and, at the other, as the 'normal' practice of underdeveloped or 'traditional' societies. In Chapter 7, we seek to move the analysis forward and, in particular, to understand the relations between the moral economy of corruption and politics – that is, how corruption is instrumentalized politically.

Chapter 8, for its part, re-examines the question of dependence and structural adjustment, ostensibly the two pillars of Africa's present links to the world economy. Here, the aim is not so much to confirm the extent to which Africa is subservient both to the export of a few primary products and to foreign aid, as it is to understand how these economic facts matter for the continent's political order. The question is whether dependence and structural adjustment have contributed to the extension of patrimonialism in Africa. If this were the case, it would help explain why there are powerful political factors working against the economic reforms demanded by Western aid donors.

The last chapter of the book raises a difficult but unavoidable question: why it is that the continent is the only one in the world to have failed significantly to develop in the last twenty-five years? If the standard interpretations stress the external constraints on African economies, there is now an increasing number of voices, many of which are African, asking whether this is not due to social, political and above all cultural factors which conspire against development as we know it. This chapter will look in some detail at what those determinants might be, how they affect Africa's economic life and how they might impinge on what we have called the instrumentalization of political disorder.

7

The (Ab)use
of Corruption

Most studies on corruption approach the question from a normative viewpoint. This is understandable as the practice is very seriously frowned upon in Western societies, and it is therefore difficult to discuss it other than in moral terms or in ways which are not analytically neutral. The typical interpretation of this phenomenon is one which refers either to the blatant absence of respect for given procedures or to a process of deliquescence – in other words, a self-evidently reprehensible deviation from a politically legitimate state of affairs.

The question becomes somewhat more complex in respect of the analysis of non-Western societies. How does one define corruption? By what standards does one assess the extent and the significance of the phenomenon? When and why is a practice considered deviant in Europe perceived similarly elsewhere? For us, the only way forward is to avoid reasoning simplistically in terms of the bureaucratic ideals which we, in the West, assume to have universal relevance.

As we have argued repeatedly, our starting point must be that the state in sub-Saharan Africa is nothing other than a relatively empty shell. For socially and culturally instrumental reasons, the real business of politics is conducted informally and, more stealthily, outside the official political realm. Within such a political 'order', in which there is little meaningful institutionalization, the notion of corruption, as habitually defined in Western polities, is of little significance. Other than from our own normative perspective, an approach based on the approved vision of the phenomenon is unlikely to further our understanding of what is actually happening on the continent.

More fruitful, we think, is an enquiry paying attention to two main considerations. First, what are the key cultural, social and psychological foundations of the mentalities which make possible such (admittedly ambivalent) practices? By focusing attention on their premises, we aim to uncover the social codes which explain how what we call corruption is most frequently bound up with important ties of reciprocity linking those who are related within networks of vertical relations. Second, we want to assess the consequences of this phenomenon at the micro- and macro-levels of society. If corruption, as it is to be observed in contemporary Africa, is often deleterious for the country as a whole, how can it remain both legitimate and practical for the actors involved?

Why corruption?

The study of corruption is beset with analytical and practical difficulties. In the first instance, it is virtually impossible to agree on a workable definition of the phenomenon. Second, there is no convenient interpretative framework which helps explain the links between the various levels (micro- and macro-) of corruption. Finally, and most obviously, it is difficult, when not downright impossible, empirically to observe the phenomenon in a scientifically meaningful way.

It is thus noticeable that most work on corruption is prefaced by convoluted discussions on issues of definition: what, in effect, is its precise meaning in different countries? This explains why there is plainly no agreed approach to the phenomenon, least of all when it comes to Africa. The result is large-scale analytical confusion, in which ethical, legal and normative precepts vie with arguments in favour of an approach based on empathy[1] for what are clearly illicit, when not illegitimate, activities.

As a result, the study of corruption in Africa has spawned a highly controversial literature in which it is obvious that many authors have sought either to defend a particular 'thesis' or to discredit other approaches taken to be unacceptable, if often for no other than ideological reasons. This is particularly apparent when it comes to the (by now) almost ritualistic discussion of the causes of the phenomenon. Two main approaches conflict. On the one hand, theories of continuity, often with an anthropological filiation, attempt to show how contemporary practices are to be explained by century-old notions of exchange. On the other hand, theories of rupture emphasize that corruption is a modern development due in large part to the erosion of

---

[1] The notion of empathy refers to the ability of the observer to place him/herself in the place of other social actors in order the better to understand their motivations and perceptions from a strictly neutral perspective.

ancestral values which took place during the colonial period and immediately after independence.

The debate is unfortunately vitiated by a most unsatisfactory opposition of principle between those observers content to rely on a stereotypical vision of Black Africa and a whole host of intellectuals looking to exculpate and redeem the continent. Each side is able without difficulty to identify the events, processes and anecdotes which support its own notion of the phenomenon. It is thus easy to form two opposite, and somewhat extremist, views. The one consists in irrevocably ostracizing the continent as a hopeless den of corruption on the basis of a blinkered and largely ahistorical interpretation lacking in self-critical awareness. The other runs the risk, in reaction, of idealizing the virtues of a pre-colonial era supposedly devoid of corruption, the growth of which is supposed to have been caused by the perversion of the social order induced by the arrival of the colonialist Europeans.

Above and beyond such largely sterile quarrels, it is important to stress that not all analytical interpretations of corruption provide equally convincing accounts of what is happening today on the continent. The developmentalist approach stresses that the phenomenon is inevitable during the modernizing phase and that it can even be seen as being functionally useful in so far as it eases the transition to institutionalization.[2] Very largely Western, this analysis rests on a dichotomy between the private and public spheres which is not to be found in Africa: it is, generally, not consistent with the evidence. Furthermore, contrary to developmentalist expectations, such kleptocratic behaviour is not confined to the first post-colonial generation of political elites taking advantage of the riches afforded by their access to power. It is in fact an integral part of the contemporary political order on the continent.[3]

Similarly, those approaches which stress either the absence of professionalism or the scarcity of resources in Africa are not wholly convincing. Corruption could conceivably be interpreted as an indication that the supply of public 'goods' cannot satisfy the demand for them – hence the illegal 'surcharge'. Yet this is a view that obscures as much as it reveals. Indeed, if corruption is merely a reflection of a transitory state of disequilibrium, how then do we explain the overwhelming evidence that it is a routine aspect of the social system? For example, it is

[2] The standard reference is the chapter on 'Modernization and Corruption' in Samuel Huntington, *Political Order in Changing Societies* (New Haven, CT: Yale University Press, 1968), where corruption is seen as preferable to violence.

[3] The controversial thesis that corruption is to be explained by the rise from poverty of such elites is put forward by S. Osaba, 'The Nigerian Power Elite, 1952, 1965' in P.C.W. Gutkind and Peter Waterman (eds), *African Social Studies* (London: Heinemann, 1976), pp. 378–9.

interesting to note that developmentalists minimize the extent of corruption at the top, simply because it does not fit well with their view of the modernizing and Westernizing elites.

Marxist or materialist approaches are no more plausible. They tend to regard corruption as an additional source of revenue, a further extraction of surplus value which exacerbates the 'exploitation of the dominated classes'. In the circumstances of Africa, however, the question arises as to whether corruption should merely be seen as a 'self-ish' additional source of income or more accurately understood as part of a complex network of redistribution driven by particularistic social pressures? 'Third-worldist' approaches thus neglect to discuss the 'corruption of survival' at the bottom of society, as it does not appear to emphasize the exploitative practices of an African bourgeoisie devoid of moral principles.

Such analytical frameworks, stressing only what seems compatible with more general social or political paradigms, and ignoring what does not fit in with them, are in the end equally unconvincing. It is not just that they largely fail to explain what is happening in Africa south of the Sahara. It is primarily because to fly in this way in the face of the evidence that corruption is both more common and less normatively clear-cut impairs our understanding of the continent. Our aim, therefore, is primarily to make sense of what we observe empirically in post-colonial Africa, regardless of ideological, normative or analytical preconceptions.

It is in this respect imperative to emphasize that the phenomenon which concerns us touches all social strata: from billionaires to the lowliest functionary. Consequently, the dichotomy between 'high' and 'low', or 'small-' and 'large-' scale, corruption is not a determinant factor in our analysis. Neither are the subtle (or not so subtle) typologies pointing to differences between financial malpractice, illegal commissions, small graft, open abuse of power, and petty pilfering, etc. Nor, finally, do we find it enlightening to attempt to discover whether some forms of corruption are more reprehensible than others.[4] However interesting a focus on differently identifiable types of illegal activities might be, it is in our view often misleading as it obscures the fact that they are all part of an interconnected whole. What is, for example, significant for us is to establish the link between, say, the Nigerian post office employee who sells stamps at a premium and the army general who arranges the filling of an oil tanker at night in exchange for a deposit in his Swiss bank account.[5]

---

[4] See Heidenheimer's work in Arnold Heidenheimer, Michael Johnston and Victor Levine, *Political Corruption: a handbook* (New Brunswick, NJ: Transaction Publishers, 1989).

[5] See here Reno, 1995.

As we have argued throughout this book, both the socio-political context and the intricacies of political practices as we observe them are best understood as deriving from a common social tradition or culture. An emphasis on horizontal social cleavages is not only a distorted view of African realities but it also leads to erroneous interpretations of those phenomena which concern us here. Similarly, distinctions between political, administrative, economic and social corruption are not as significant as they might at first appear. What matters is that everywhere on the continent both political success and economic prosperity require considerable 'investment': it is necessary to convince the indispensable 'intermediaries' of one's potential by showing greater 'generosity' than one's competitors. Given the difficulty of getting resources, it is easy to understand why predatory practices remain one of the main ways of obtaining the means of meeting such obligations, whatever one's position in society.

We must also confront squarely the question of how to compare corruption in Africa with that prevailing in our own countries. Even if it is wise not to be naive about the extent to which the Western legal-rational bureaucratic practices have managed to eradicate graft,[6] it is proper to point to the differences both of kind and degree with what happens on the African continent,[7] where corruption is not just endemic but an integral part of the social fabric of life. For those at the bottom end of society, like lowly civil servants, the sale of the limited amount of power they possess is virtually their only means of survival. Higher up, extortion is one of the major avenues of enrichment; it facilitates social advancement and the upholding of one's position. As we have seen, it enables the political elites to fulfil their duties, to meet the expectations of their clients and, hence, to enhance their status.

Provided the beneficiaries of graft do not hoard too much of what they accumulate by means of the exploitation of the resources made available to them through their position, and provided they redistribute along lines that are judged to be socially desirable, their behaviour is deemed acceptable. Corruption is not, therefore, a matter of a few 'rotten apples' or of a venal 'class', even less an 'evil' to be eradicated by means of vigorous 'ethical' campaigns. On the contrary, it is a habitual part of everyday life, an expected element of every social transaction. This ought not to surprise us. As we have already emphasized, there is in Africa a marked reluctance to abide by the abstract and universalist norms of the legal-bureaucratic order that are the foundations of Western polities. The legitimacy of the formal rules of conduct which

---

[6] One may read with interest what is undoubtedly a subtle interpretation in Theobald, 1990.

[7] A difference which some find difficult to accept: see Jean-François Bayart, 'L'historicité de l'Etat importé', *loc. cit.*, pp. 33–4.

characterize the modern state has hitherto failed to supersede that of the informal compacts derived from ethnic, factional, or nepotistic ties of solidarity.

This may explain why there is in Africa very little serious censure of corruption so long as its fruits are deemed to have been suitably and vigorously redistributed according to the logic of patronage. Condemnation is reserved for those individuals or groups (like some military cliques) who are seen to appropriate 'public' resources purely out of greed and with little regard for those who would count on bene-fiting from such graft. As the much lamented Ken Saro-Wiwa noted with his usual incisiveness, supporters will readily applaud when one of their own political leaders appropriates millions in the capital city but will at the same time expect him to be scrupulously honest in the management of his village finances.[8] Expectations of probity, therefore, appear to be limited to one's kith and kin, the members of one's com-munity, but they obviously cease to apply beyond. The usual response by Nigerians to the charge that their country is deemed by some to be the most corrupt on earth is: 'This is how we do things in Nigeria!'[9]

Consequently, an examination of such practices in terms of moral disapproval or of an African pathology is bound to lead to an analytical dead end, since it would be based either on a coarse external approach or a misleading standpoint. It is, however, much more fruitful to study this phenomenon as a properly grounded 'moral economy of corrup-tion', that is, an enquiry into behavioural patterns which are embedded in the dominant social imperatives.[10] It then becomes possible to understand how seemingly dishonest attitudes are, in large measure at least, the result of particularistic and communitarian codes of conduct which have little in common with the notion of the public good.

This, in turn, makes clear how much of what is happening in contemporary Africa follows on from the norms and practices of the pre-colonial period. Indeed, such factors as the obligations of mutual support, the imperatives of reciprocity, the importance of gift exchange, the payment of tribute, the need to redistribute, even the habits of cattle rustling or, more generally, of plundering others, all

---

[8] Ken Saro-Wiwa, 1991. Saro-Wiwa was hanged, following a show trial, by the Abacha junta at the end of 1995.

[9] We refer here to the corruption league table established by the organization Transparency International, through surveys of the opinions of businessmen. Although of limited value, such an annual exercise is at least useful for compara-tive purposes over time.

[10] See here Olivier de Sardan, 1996, who analyses the links between corruption and such important social practices as negotiation, exchange, reciprocity and redistrib-ution. See also Hyden, 1980.

have a bearing on the phenomenon of corruption on the continent today.[11] Let us enter an important caveat here: we are not putting forward an outdated 'cultural' interpretation of present-day Africa. We are merely highlighting those aspects of that 'moral economy of corruption' which are best explained by the successful adaptation of existing social practices to the demands of a modern economy (larger markets, the use of paper money, modern telecommunications, etc.).

We are not dealing with antiquated practices on their way to extinction but, much more realistically, with codes of conduct which are at the heart of modern economic activities. Even those Africans who support wholeheartedly the principles of economic development and the reforms inspired by the Bretton Woods institutions are not in a position to operate outside such social rules and imperatives. Hence, what we are inclined to label as corruption is in reality a complex of behavioural patterns which are key ingredients of the continent's modernity. Indeed, as we explain elsewhere in the book, Africa is modernizing but according to a developmental logic which is only superficially akin to the Western model and which we are only now beginning to understand.

Corruption: from dysfunctionality to instrumentality

There is a large body of work that seeks to assess both the scope and the effects of corruption on the economies of the continent. It is, as one would expect, an exacting task, involving at times complicated mathematical models, but one which is rarely useful to the student of comparative politics. All such evaluation rests on one simple and fundamental question: how does one measure the extent of the phenomenon? Are we to look at the size of illegal payments, the measure of the informal economy, or at the extent of corruption as a proportion of a country's official GDP? The emphasis on actual figures makes little sense outside the context of the nation's economic resources and wealth: the appropriation of $1,000 million may be insignificant in an oil-producing state, whereas the disappearance of $200 million might cripple the exchequer of a low-income resourceless country.

Furthermore, there is a tendency to concentrate attention on wrongdoing at the top, as if such practices were confined to the polit-

---

[11] Monday Ekpo, who has compiled a useful list of such factors, points to continuities in the causes of corruption in his article 'Gift-Giving Practices and Bureaucratic Corruption in Nigeria', published in *Bureaucratic Corruption in Sub-Saharan Africa: toward a search for causes and consequences* (Washington, DC: University Press of America, 1979). See also Guy Nicolas' remarkable 1987 study.

ical and economic elites. However, it is clear that such conduct is to
be found at every level in society and affects in this way the whole
range of financial and commercial transactions in Africa. Indeed, in a
situation where the systematic pilfering of public resources is habitual, the sum total of such innumerable and apparently negligible
individual actions can be as detrimental to the country's economy as
large scale corruption at the top.

In sub-Saharan Africa, corruption is rarely centralized: everyone
everywhere tries to benefit. Examples abound: in airports, each official
(passport, health, customs, baggage, etc.) wants his/her cut, making
progress to the exit an obstacle course. Driving from Lagos to Cotonou,
for instance, the traveller is likely to encounter at least a dozen road
blocks, manned by different police forces, various army corps, flying
customs officers, local authority officials, etc., each duplicating the
same control of papers and documents – less, let us be clear, in the interest of safety than of extracting revenue from their power to obstruct further progress down the road. In other words, there is no arrangement
between these miscellaneous functionaries, no agreement as to the payment that would ensure the unofficial laissez-passer or otherwise
deliver the required authorization. There is, as it were, no one-off payment but, instead, an interminable series of negotiations with an end-
less number of petty officials.

More importantly, there is little evidence in Africa of the type of 'horizontal' corruption that is not infrequently found in our own societies
– meaning here the exchange of favours between economic and political elites. In the West, as in other developed countries, such practices
generally occur at the top, where deals are struck between, on the one
hand, the main industrial and financial sectors and, on the other, the
political classes. This collusion between important economic actors
and politicians results, for example, in the exchange of profitable
favours (most notably in respect of the acquisition of land and construction contracts) for the illegal financing of political parties.

By contrast, corruption in Africa concerns the whole of the population and operates essentially according to vertical relations of inequality. It is not confined to given sectors of economic activity, even if the
'purchase' of favours within certain key administrative areas (most particularly connected with the control of trade licences) or in some highly
sensitive geographical areas (such as borders) is obviously highly desirable. In truth, access to the right people in such circumstances can be
richly rewarding. Outside one's own community (however loosely
defined), where rules of civic behaviour apply, there is an assumption
that graft presides over all forms of exchange. Conversely, those who do
not show themselves sufficiently munificent following their appoint-

ment to public office are *ipso facto* deemed to be 'suspicious'. They are seen as either inept or selfish – neither of which is deemed acceptable.

Our argument is that, even if such practices are nefarious to the macro- 'development' of African countries, since it makes rational economic activity practically impossible, there are good reasons why they are not likely to disappear. Indeed, a system of such profound uncertainty and disorder, if not opaqueness, which depends on subtle and constantly fluctuating ties of loyalty, provides ample opportunity for the instrumental use of properly cultivated social relations. This, in turn, raises the question of whether such complex informal arrangements, such well-organized predatory networks, do not actually conspire to create and maintain a system of legitimization based on unequal exchange which lies at the very heart of the political 'order'.

The history of the post-colonial (neo-)patrimonial society shows that such a strategy of prebendal exploitation is mutually profitable, provided those who profit redistribute appropriately. African states would undoubtedly stand to benefit from a more regulated economy, but the main political and economic elites are able to use the absence of transparency as a most valuable resource. Such is the efficacy of the existing system that it has survived unscathed all generational and social change, adapting as it goes along to the demands of modernity. In an environment where informal compacts weigh more than institutional regulations, where public opinion legitimizes the right kind of personalized exchange, venality can thrive and evolve over time. Given the durability of vertical social relations and the endurance of certain forms of political representation, corruption remains instrumentally rational.

Our analysis of the phenomenon, therefore, demonstrates how (yet again) the understanding of what may appear to be a peculiarly pathological African condition is in reality nothing other than a specific aspect of what is utterly judicious behaviour in the circumstances. Empirically as well as analytically, corruption is best explained as one key aspect of the instrumentalization of disorder. It is, however, crucial to note how the processes under scrutiny are interconnected. As we have stressed, those who seek political support need to nourish infranational networks of patronage if they are to succeed, or even survive, as legitimized 'representatives'. At the same time, such benefaction must remain personalized, ever renegotiable, and asymmetrical.

A well-regulated system of political transactions, operating within the ambit of a bureaucratic welfare state and the rule of law, would make impossible the type of personalized complex of clientelism on which political legitimacy rests. Given that the state in Africa is not, and will not in the foreseeable future be, in a position to garner the resources needed for an egalitarian distribution of resources according to social needs, (neo-)patrimonialism continues to suit both patrons and clients. Consequently, corruption can be seen as the outcome of a number of interconnected phenomena feeding logically off each other and in which the search for political status nourishes a scheme by which power and authority are constantly negotiated and purchased.

It is for this reason that the prospect for institutionalization is illusory. The dominance of unofficial forms of exchange as well as the absence of bureaucratic professionalism merely buttress the informalization of politics. There is little scope for the sedimentation of a truly national political order on the Western model. The very dynamics of the system foster the continuation of vertical (communitarian, nepotistic or clientelistic) social relations and contribute to the creative blurring of the boundaries between the public and private spheres, both of which are uncommonly favourable to the flowering of corruption. As we have noted, such a state of affairs may not be desirable in the long term for the country as a whole, but it remains both entirely coherent and eminently reasonable for those Africans who can manage to benefit from the system as it *works*.

It will no doubt be argued that corruption is rarely condoned and, even, that it is frequently condemned in countries, like Nigeria, where it has reached gargantuan proportions. Officially, all African societies have accepted Western norms in respect of this phenomenon, which is why the local press regularly exposes the most blatant cases of venality and illegal deals. However, above and beyond such ritual disclosure of wrongdoing and the no less ceremonial demand for the upholding of the rule of law, it is well to ask whether this denunciation is not essentially instrumental. We would argue that, with few exceptions, such anti-corruption discourse is primarily rhetorical and that the recurrent purges which follow are, more often than not, convenient devices for eliminating political rivals rather than a real attempt to reform the political 'order'.

The major anti-corruption campaigns undertaken by Kountché in Niger, Eyadema in Togo, or Traoré in Mali, however well-meaning, have not resulted in a systemic overhaul of these countries' polities. This is also true of Nigeria, where virtually all regimes have launched propaganda operations in support of greater probity. Can it be seriously argued that the 'Ethical Revolution' under the Second Republic, Buhari's 'War against Indiscipline' or Babangida's 'Mass Mobilization for Self-Reliance' and 'Economic Recovery and Justice', have in any way modified the rules of the political game in that key West African nation? Here, as elsewhere, an apparent adherence to the Western values currently in force across the world merely serves to obscure the perpetuation of the selfsame informal political norms. In truth, a careful empirical study of the reality surrounding the publicity about corruption scandals on the continent shows that such charges are invariably deployed as political instruments. They do not indicate in-depth institutional changes.

It is revealing in this respect that even in countries noted for their successful 'transition to democracy', very little has changed. In Zambia, for example, the change of regime, from Kaunda to Chiluba, has not reduced either the frequency or the depth of such political exactions: hence the gap between the image of a 'secure' and reformed Zambia projected abroad and the reality on the ground. The realization of the scale of current misdeeds has been a severe disappointment to major aid donors (like Japan or the Scandinavian countries) who now recognize that much of their assistance has been 'mislaid'. But Western countries do not seriously contemplate sanctions, even if they protest and at times freeze their aid programmes, precisely because Zambia is supposed to have been one of the beacons of the present 'transitions' on the continent. Although there is today some disappointment at the lack of 'democratic' political change south of the Sahara, Africa continues to receive massive assistance from the major Western donors. Aid fatigue has not yet set in.

The mistaken assumption that 'democratic transitions' would *ipso facto* reduce corruption derives mainly, we would argue, from our inability to understand its structural, social and cultural roots. Democratic reform on the Western model – that is the political institutionalization of the bureaucratic and legal order – would undoubtedly have brought about greater accountability, more transparency and a more effective system of checks and balances. However, and despite changes to the façade of governance, the introduction of multi-party elections into Africa has not yet had the desired effects. In reality, not much has changed.

It is also becoming increasingly plain that economic liberalization, and its attendant reduction in the resources available in the public sector, has not contributed to a lessening of corruption. The most recent studies on this subject would highlight instead the adaptation of corrupt practices to the new economic climate.[12] What has happened in Africa, as we explained in our chapter on the Illusions of Civil Society, is merely a change of strategy, moving away from the state and giving greater prominence to the market and to NGOs. Corruption, as it were, has been decentralized. Indeed, a closer examination of the evidence would reveal that a large number of key political actors have now shifted their operations to the local level, which currently enjoys wide international favour and receives substantial assistance. There is, however, no indication that such mutation has

[12] For a discussion of this topic see, for instance, the *Institute of Development Studies Bulletin*, 27 (2) (April 1996).

induced significant change in the link between enrichment and political legitimacy.

A comparative analysis of corruption (which at this stage can be no other than Eurocentric) shows that both the nature of the sedimentation of the state and the texture of a society's political culture are more telling indicators than the complexion of a regime or of its economic system. Corruption is not a hallmark of authoritarianism; nor is it (as we are now well aware) incompatible with democratic systems. This is not to say, as some might mischievously deduce, that Africa's political culture is especially propitious to corruption; our argument is merely that it is instrumentally profitable in the present circumstances. But why eschew a discussion of political culture for fear of being misunderstood, when we know that such considerations are entirely relevant to the understanding of politics worldwide?

It is plain for example, that in some European countries like Sweden or the Netherlands, social and cultural constraints go against the devotion to personal enrichment. In such settings, the revelation of the slightest venal misdeed is fatal to the career of politicians. Elsewhere, as in Belgium or many Mediterranean countries, prevalent norms and customs are far more tolerant of illicit practices and politicians not infrequently function at the limits of legality. Hence, any well-grounded analysis must consider how different notions of public accountability impinge on the fabric of political legitimacy and efficacy in Western Europe as in Africa. And while it may be rash to generalize about the whole of the continent, we believe it is reasonable to suggest that in Africa south of the Sahara the informalization of politics is instrumentally linked to corruption. It is, of course, understandable why Nigerians, for instance, are exasperated at the publicity generated by their status as the world's most corrupt nation. Nor is it surprising that they should readily argue that it is the same everywhere, implying thereby that no one (not even in developed countries) is in a position to lecture them on the matter. Yet such comforting universalist generalizations do not really hold.

Normative considerations aside, what is clear is that corruption is not in and of itself inimical to economic growth, as is amply demonstrated by the experience of Japan and the other so-called Asian tigers. The puzzle about Africa is why there has been so little development. To paraphrase a Chinese metaphor, in Asia corruption has lubricated the economic machine whereas in Africa it has made it seize up. To explain this dissimilarity is not easy, since it is necessary to take a

---

[13] We draw here on a certain number of arguments outlined in Jean-Pascal Daloz and Man Ho Heo, 'La corruption en Corée du Sud et au Nigéria: pistes de recherche comparatives', *Revue internationale de politique comparée*, 4 (2)(September 1997), a special issue with several articles relevant to the present chapter.

wide array of different factors into account. We attempt here merely to sketch a broad comparative canvas.[13]

The key question undoubtedly is: what happens to the proceeds of corruption? Clearly, in Africa, much more than in Asia, a significant proportion is devoted to the provision of the required largesse, since it is expected that those who occupy prestigious and highly remunerative positions will contribute to the collective prestige of their community. Above and beyond the immediate family, for which they have direct responsibility, the wealthy are meant to contribute to the upkeep of the extended network of blood relatives, meeting a wide range of expenses, among others those associated with births, marriages, funerals, education, cults of ancestors, etc.

The maintenance of the wider circle of their entourage and, beyond, of unrelated clients, is the next priority. Rank, prestige and, above all, legitimacy will be proportional to the extension of the clientelistic circle. Those who fail to redistribute, or are perceived to redistribute too little, run the risk of facing hostility and suspicion.[14] They will not receive recognition and deference. Within such a context, it is evident that the elites expend huge amounts of money, a situation inherently conducive to corruption – even if the main purpose of such kleptocracy is not so much personal enrichment as the nourishment of one's popularity.

This being the case, it is important to point to a singularly significant distinction between Africa and Asia. South of the Sahara, above and beyond the munificence discussed above, little is re-invested productively at the local or national level. Wealth is spent primarily on luxury or prestige goods. Yet, and this is crucial, the display of opulence does not derive simply from the need to exhibit social prominence. Ostentation is also, and perhaps primarily, an important way of meeting the clientelistic need for 'wonderment' before the patron and, as such, it can likewise be seen as a political resource. It makes good political sense to act as a *bon viveur*, to flaunt one's substance, to spend abundantly and instantly, without worrying about the future. As for the most sizeable African fortunes, they are usually put safely away in European or North American investment banks, a logical move, given the suspicion shown towards local financial institutions. In other words, they are of remarkably little use to African economies.

On the other hand, in countries like South Korea, not only is there a high degree of trust in local banking establishments but the spiriting of funds abroad is considered akin to a betrayal of one's obliga-

[14] See here the range of African proverbs pointing to the ephemeral nature of power and the need to take full advantage of its tenure, but always with the caveat that it must be shared with one's 'dependants'. One of many: 'Whoever does not rob the state robs his kith and kin'.

tions to the nation. Instead, various devices of dubious legality are used to deposit 'dirty' money into *bona fide* bank accounts. The phenomenon is so widespread that recent reforms have compelled banks to provide more information about their customers' accounts. The result, however, has not been the widespread transfer of funds abroad but, rather, the hoarding of money at home. Here, the tendency to save locally can in effect be seen as a 'nationalist' reflex. Whatever the case, corruption in South Korea does not entail the movement of capital overseas, a factor which is obviously favourable to investment in the local economy.[15]

Furthermore, if material prosperity has always been admired in Asia, an excess of opulence is often considered to be in bad taste. It would be unthinkable to spend in South Korea only a fraction of what the elites are prepared to disburse on ostentation in Nigeria – even if there is today a slight movement in that direction. As in Japan, the consumption of luxury goods has naturally grown along with the general rise in prosperity. Nevertheless, the recent crisis has shown how quickly opulence is jettisoned (at least officially) when the country's economy is seen to have weakened: the sight of Koreans donating their gold jewellery to help sustain the nation's balance of payments is revealing in this respect. Already in 1990, the Korean government had launched a campaign of frugality. Without reading too much into these public displays of economic 'nationalism', it stands to reason that such differences of attitude are undoubtedly one of the factors explaining why productive investment is higher in Asia than in Africa.

Africa is, obviously, not uniquely prone to corruption, even if its practice is notoriously widespread. What is true is that it is more visible than elsewhere, as though its prominence did not constitute a serious problem for Africans. By contrast, discretion is imperative in the Far East, where the total amounts involved in illicit activities are undoubtedly larger than they are on the African continent. In Africa, there is a distinct impression that corruption remains accepted as an integral part of the socio-political order above and beyond the official discourse which decries the practice and the occasional campaigns set up to deal with this apparent 'scourge'. The question arises, therefore, whether, in the absence of genuine reform, the continent will not increasingly become involved in illegal international trade, made eas-

---

[15] It is not clear whether the acute economic crisis faced by South Korea and most other Asian countries invalidates the remarks made above. It has certainly revealed some of the most perverse consequences of the cosy arrangements between economic conglomerates, banking institutions and the political elites. At the time of writing, however, economists are in disagreement as to how structurally significant the crisis is likely to be.

ier by the absence of meaningful regulations and the connivance of the authorities concerned.

It is indeed possible that some parts of sub-Saharan Africa will evolve into centres of an economy similar to that found in the north of Burma or in some Colombian cities. It is unlikely, however, that it will see the rise of highly structured and ruthlessly efficient criminal organizations (on the model of the Italian-American Mafia, Chinese Triads or Japanese Yaks) which require a higher degree of formal management skills than those currently found in Africa. The aim on the continent is to seek gradually to informalize all sectors of the economy, not merely to operate within the ambit of the parallel sector developed at the margin of the political centres. In such an environment there are undoubtedly profits to be made, both to sustain the enrichment of the elites and to support their clients. Whether such practices are compatible with macro-economic growth and, even more, with development as it is generally understood in the West, is a question to which we shall return in due course.

8

The Bounties of Dependence

The question of dependence has long been at the heart of the analysis of Africa's economic predicament, even if the arguments of under-development and dependency theory no longer carry the same conviction.[1] It is generally accepted that the continent's reliance on the exports of a few primary products, its lack of competitiveness, its vulnerability to the price fluctuation of essential imports and its marginalization in the world economy all militate against its development potential. It is also agreed that Africa now suffers from an unsustainable debt burden.

In this chapter, we reconsider the facts of dependence to see whether this apparently deleterious situation has not in reality been used with profit by those who hold power and their numerous clients. Presented in this way, the question may appear provocative but it can no longer merely be assumed that foreign aid simply and accurately reflects the basic needs of countries which are too poor to survive – even if that is true in some cases. Nor can it be accepted at face value that dependence is 'nefarious' – even if it turns out to be detrimental to what we conceive of as economic development.[2] Even less, finally, can reliance on foreign aid be considered 'temporary'.

Both the degree and role of foreign assistance ought to be examined from a less normative and more firmly analytical point of view. In the real world, it seems clear that dependence is a structural condition of African countries and that it has become an integral part of the workings of their economic and political systems. What this means is that

---

[1] For a more systematic discussion of dependence see Chabal, 1992: Chapter 14.
[2] The extent to which aid is detrimental to development or how it may even be inimical to the well-being of the poor it is intending to help is an issue we do not discuss here. See de Waal, 1997.

dependence is to be conceptualized simultaneously as a constraint and as a resource. It is a constraint in that it imposes economic and political conditions on the granting and use of foreign aid, although many of these are ignored or evaded. It is a resource in that it furnishes the recipient state with financial means it would not otherwise possess.

The assumption, therefore, that dependence is *ipso facto* damaging to African countries cannot be maintained. Instead, the political analyst of Africa must examine the genesis and mechanisms of the phenomenon with an eye to understanding better how it has become an integral part of the political economy of contemporary Africa. Here we want to focus more specifically on two key aspects of dependence: the first has to do with the ways in which foreign aid has been instrumentalized by ruling elites over time; the second is concerned with an analysis of the effects of structural adjustment programmes on African countries today.

Dependence as resource

The most fruitful way to conceptualize dependence is to link it with the workings of the political system prevailing south of the Sahara. Dependence is not an extraneous aspect of Africa's economic and political condition; it is intrinsic to the very operation of the continent's political economy. The history of Africa's dependence, therefore, is intimately tied to the development of the patrimonial political order. Right from independence, African elites have conceived of their economic links with the outside world – whether in the form of the export of their raw materials or aid from the former colonial power – as an integral part of their calculus for power. African rulers have never contemplated a future for the continent divorced from the external economic links which were eventually labelled as 'dependence', on the models of neo-colonialism or neo-imperialism outlined by scholars like Emmanuel Arghiri and Samir Amin.[3]

Not only has dependence been an integral part of Africa's political economy but its relative importance to the continent has increased over time. Far from seeking to free themselves from the international economy and the world of aid donors, most African governments have sought ever greater external economic investment in, and financial aid to, their countries.[4] Although it is probably fair to say that no African regime bargained for the present punitive constraints imposed by

[3] See Emmanuel Arghiri, *L'échange inégal* (Paris: Maspéro, 1969) and Samir Amin, *Le développement inégal* (Paris: Editions de Minuit, 1973).
[4] Though there were in the 1970s a few countries, like Zambia for instance, which sought to develop import substitution industries in order to be less dependent on outside multinationals. These attempts were not successful and did not survive the economic crisis which followed.

structural adjustment, it remains the case that many of them developed strategies for instrumentalizing dependence politically to their advantage. We want in this section to examine in greater detail: (1) the genesis of dependence; (2) the management of dependence; and (3) the politics of dependence.

(a) The genesis of dependence. The origins of dependence lie in three distinct areas: the continuation of the economic connections with the former colonial powers; the place of Africa's economies in the world trade system; and the growth in international borrowing.

Two interrelated factors ensured the overriding importance of the economic links with the former colonial power: extensive and public for the francophone countries, more diffuse and private for the former British colonies. First, at independence African governments had inbuilt expectations of extensive bilateral foreign aid. Whether in the form of direct grants or in terms of capital investment, such bilateral support – a continuation of the especially heavy financial commitments which the colonial governments made in the decade before independence – was always a vital component of the national accounts. Second, there quickly emerged a crucial connection between foreign aid and foreign policy. In other words, African rulers became accustomed to negotiating their political support of the former colonial power (or indeed other Western or Eastern governments) in exchange for foreign aid.

Whilst it is perhaps most obvious how these dynamics were engendered and nourished within the former French African empire, since France was so blatant in the exploitation of its African clients for purposes of international relations, similar processes were also discernible elsewhere in Africa. Indeed, in many ways the Commonwealth provided an ideal, if admittedly looser, framework for the maintenance of links between the UK and Africa which, in more subtle ways, rivalled those of the French. Furthermore, for specific historical and economic reasons, some African countries – like Zaire, Nigeria, Gabon – were able to forge special connections with a number of Western countries (Belgium, France, the UK, Germany, Italy, the Netherlands and the US) almost immediately after independence.

The point here is not so much to compare the extent of the influence of the former colonial masters in Africa but to understand how such patterns of international relations formalized the use of foreign aid as a political instrument. Outside powers were willing to offer aid as a means of purchasing client states in Africa. Conversely, African elites considered foreign aid as one of their negotiable commodities. Both sides knew that foreign aid was politically open to bargaining and it became in this way one of the most dependable economic resources available to African governments. How foreign aid was negotiated and how it was utilized internally are two issues we examine below.

The second reason for Africa's dependence – its place in the world trade system – derived naturally from the fact that, during the colonial period, the continent was primarily a supplier of raw materials and agricultural products to the imperial centres and beyond. Although there never was a realistic option that, after independence, African countries could afford not to exploit to the full the export of such products, the question is whether African governments pursued policies likely to maximize the use of their resources for the purpose of sustained development. The short answer is that they did not. With very few exceptions (like Botswana and, perhaps, Gabon), African governments simply exploited their economic assets for patrimonial (or prebendal) purposes, regardless of the consequences of such actions for the country's future economic well-being.

This was evident in at least two ways. The first is that ruling elites took a short-term economic view, seeking to maximize returns immediately rather than invest for future development. Perhaps because they were insecure about their own tenure of power or perhaps because they needed these resources in order to expand their patrimonial networks fast, they continued to rely for revenues on the export of their traditional crops or minerals, thus merely increasing their country's dependence on outside markets. The second is that they did not seriously pursue policies likely to diversify their economies, and thereby lessen their reliance on single exports. To have done that would have required high capital investment and deferred profits. Far from seizing the opportunity of reducing dependence, African rulers have tended largely to maximize revenue from the export of existing resources, at the expense of diversification and sometimes even at the expense of the continued production of their main exports.

Although in the long run such short-term policies were bound to be counter-productive for Africa, the continent's elites were relentless in the pursuit of immediate gains. And indeed, one of the reasons why supposedly responsible governments could get away with policies that jeopardized the economic well-being of the countries over which they presided is because they remained confident of continued foreign aid. Thus, for example, most West African governments followed short-term export-oriented rural policies which eventually damaged their countries' food-producing potential. Rulers simply assumed that they would be able to obtain foreign aid to counter the effects of food shortages. On the whole, their presumption turned out to be right as aid donors have always responded positively to requests for food – even if, in the harsh environment of the 1980s a number of nasty famines developed, especially in the Horn of Africa, as a result of highly irresponsible government policies.

This brings us to the third cause of dependence: excessive debt. Why did African governments borrow well above their countries' means? Historically, there are two reasons for Africa's indebtedness. One is linked with the severe economic downturn precipitated in the 1970s by the rise in oil prices as well as of manufactured imported goods and with the gradual fall in the price of most of Africa's exports. The other has to do with the ready availability of bilateral foreign aid and the willingness of private financial institutions to provide loans. Borrowing was thus seen at the time as a reasonable way of overcoming what appeared simply to be a conjunctural economic crisis. Here too, short-term policy-making was the norm: the aim was to get financial resources into Africa as quickly as possible.

Of course, Africa was not the only part of the world to become massively indebted in the 1970s; Latin American countries were borrowing even more heavily. There are, however, two aspects of the African case which are quite distinct. First, there seemed little recognition that, given Africa's declining economic standing in the world, the cost of borrowing was likely soon to be crippling. Second, and more generally, there appeared to be a belief among African governments that borrowing was akin to foreign aid: not loans with stringent conditions attached but rather just another means of transferring money to poor countries. The question of the repayment of debt did not weigh heavily on their minds, perhaps because it appeared that even excessively ambitious and economically dubious loans were easily granted by lending institutions. Many African rulers, therefore, simply assumed that they would not in practice have to repay these loans – not, as it turned out, an unreasonable assumption since private lenders had no reliable mechanism for recovering debts from bankrupt exchequers.

The consequence was that Africa's governments did not hesitate to continue to borrow as much and as often as they could. Their first, and perhaps only, priority was to ensure that the state was in receipt of the largest amount of foreign funding possible, regardless of whether it was composed of grants or loans. Thus, in the period which preceded world austerity and the imposition of structural adjustment programmes, there developed a situation in which both borrowers and lenders conspired to allow debt in Africa to soar, in breach of the financial criteria which govern lending. Above and beyond the economic need to borrow, however, it would appear that African rulers sought to multiply loan commitments so as to ensure that national lending institutions would continue to have a stake in the financial viability of their countries.

(b) The management of dependence. Although it is customary to think of those who are dependent as the victims of an unequal economic relationship on which they have little purchase, the realities of post-colonial Africa are rather different. As is perhaps best illustrated by the question of debt, African rulers have managed since independence to devise successful strategies for the transfer of funds to the states over which they preside. The debate about dependence is not whether such transfers were beneficial to the 'development' of African countries, as in most instances they obviously were not. Nor is it about whether donor countries did find ways of extracting from Africa far more than was ever given in the first place, which they did. Our argument here is simply to stress that such transfers provided African states with a much higher level of financial resources than they would otherwise have possessed. Dependence was thus one of the chief instruments which enabled African elites to obtain the means to continue to feed the patrimonial systems on which their power rested.

The management of dependence involved two complementary aspects: maximizing foreign aid and minimizing constraints on its use. Although often largely bereft of political clout, we would argue that African rulers have been supremely adept at utilizing the instruments which they did possess in order to turn dependence to their profit. Where (as in Nigeria, Angola, Gabon) they have had seriously negotiable economic assets, like oil or uranium, they have used these to the fullest possible effect, as was most notably the case with the sale of uranium to fuel France's ambitious nuclear energy programme. Where, as in the majority of cases, they have had few such resources to offer, they have sought to extract foreign aid by exploiting the weaknesses of, and the divisions between, their main potential donors. This has required the ability to manipulate the real and symbolic significance of their role as client states in the face of a world in which international relations were changing continuously.

The first and most obvious strategy was to negotiate aid with the former colonial power in exchange for international support, notably in the United Nations. Thus, France's notion of post-imperial *grandeur* was upheld by the many ways it could demonstrate that it had supportive 'client' states in Africa.[5] Similarly, Britain's notion of its post-imperial role was buttressed by the admittedly more discreet coterie of African states which belonged to the Commonwealth.

The second foreign policy strategy consisted in playing off potential patrons one against the other. Thus, African regimes like those of Zaire

---

[5] What is called in France the *'pré carré'*. For a recent view on French policy in Africa, see Chris Alden, 'From Policy Autonomy to Policy Integration: the evolution of France's role in Africa' in Chris Alden and Jean-Pascal Daloz (eds), *Paris, Pretoria and the African Continent: the international relations of states and societies in transition* (London: Macmillan, 1996).

could court several of Africa's former colonial powers and other Western countries, deploying in each case the argument which most favoured aid. France's unremitting desire to secure as many client states as possible in Africa readily encouraged the former colonies of other imperial powers (like Portugal, Belgium or even Britain) to extract foreign aid from Paris in exchange for a recognition of French 'influence' in Africa. One might point here to France's controversial aid to Biafra or to the Rwandan regime in 1994. Other examples would include support for the former Portuguese colony of Guinea Bissau to join the Franc Zone, itself an economic framework which provides its members with a convertible currency and the means to borrow easily, or Mozambique's recent accession to the Commonwealth.

The third, and perhaps most profitable, instrument for the management of foreign aid was the exploitation of Cold War rivalries.[6] Here African governments could fruitfully negotiate their adherence to East or West, and many were the advantages of such affiliations.[7] If, again, Zaire provides the archetypal example of a state able to benefit massively from its links with the West, largely for reasons having to do with the threat of disorder in Central Africa which the withholding of foreign aid might have entailed, there are many other examples of profitable Cold War calculus on the continent. Of these we shall highlight only two: the construction of the Volta dam by the Russians in Ghana and the building by the Chinese of the Tanzania-Zambia railway. During most of the 1960s and 1970s it can safely be said that African states had little difficulty in finding aid donors who imposed very few constraints on the use of foreign aid.

What is most noticeable during the period between independence and the fall of the Berlin Wall in 1989 is the extent to which African governments were successful in maximizing aid and minimizing constraints. Despite overwhelming evidence that foreign aid was rarely put to the use for which it was intended, there were precious few sanctions against such failings. Donors – whether private or public, bilateral or multilateral – seem on the whole to have accepted a degree of non-compliance with the stated aims of aid and a level of failure of targeted aid projects which beggar belief. Whether they did so out of compassion or out of narrow political and commercial interests, we are compelled to note that such a situation facilitated the extent to which African ruling elites were able to use foreign aid primarily as an additional source of clientelistic revenue.

[6] See here Zaki Laïdi, *The Superpowers and Africa: the constraints of a rivalry, 1960–1990* (Chicago: Chicago University Press, 1990).
[7] Within the general Cold War rivalry, other more limited antagonisms – China versus Taiwan, West versus East Germany, Israel versus the Arab world – could be utilized to good effect by African governments.

The end of the Cold War and the apparent triumph of liberal ideo-logies have drastically altered the international context in which Africa is seeking to manage its present dependence. Furthermore, the West's economic difficulties (notably rising unemployment) and the need to support the collapsed economies of the former Eastern Bloc countries have radically reduced the amount of financial aid which most Western countries are prepared to allocate to Africa. There is, too, a new will, or at least a proclaimed will, to make African governments more accountable both to their own population and to aid donors. Finally, the age of bilateral aid has faded, as most countries now adhere to World Bank lending principles. In practical terms, the two most significant changes which impinge today on the ability of African states to receive foreign aid are the constraints of structural adjustment and the new democratic political agenda. We discuss structural adjust-ment in the next section. We focus here on the political aspects of the new world order.

(c) The politics of dependence. The means by which African rulers have managed dependence are various but they are part of an overall strategy which has its roots in the colonial period and which one of us has called 'the politics of the mirror'.[8] This consists essentially in addressing the foreign 'other' – in this case, potential aid donors – in the language that is most congenial and, crucially, most easily rein-forces the belief that they (outsiders) understand what Africa needs. Thus it was that Africans conspired to support the colonial notion that they were all divided into discrete and identifiable 'tribes' and, later, convinced their colonial masters that they intended to run the politics of their newly independent countries on the principles of multi-party parliamentary systems. Thus it was too that some African leaders became overnight the proponents of scientific socialism or adhered wholeheartedly to the proposals for development projects which came their way.

The point here is not to approach this question from a normative standpoint but rather to understand better how it was that African rulers were able to manipulate international politics to their advan-tage. That they were able to do so with such success is connected to two important factors. First, in the post-colonial period they were in a position to benefit from the sense of collective 'shame' from which many Western countries, most notably the former imperial powers and the US, suffered in respect of the manner in which they had mal-treated the peoples of Africa and, more generally, the so-called Third World. There clearly was a 'guilt' capital which African governments

[8] Chabal, 1996.

were able to utilize to maximum effect. Second, during the Cold War, both East and West sought in general to maximize the number of their client states.

Nevertheless, and this is what we wish to emphasize here, the ability to exploit successfully the condition of dependence for the purpose of generating foreign aid must be seen as an unalloyed diplomatic achievement on the part of African politicians. The argument that Africa's crisis is primarily the result of its subservient economic status does not withstand serious examination. Africa's crisis is the combined outcome of the weakening of its patrimonial system and of the dereliction of political accountability. And the weakening of the patrimonial system is entirely due to the diminution in the internal and external resources to feed it. Of the two, the internal is the more dramatic, making the need for increased foreign aid and investment (or, precisely, increased dependence) all the more vital. But, in the post-Cold War context, there are a number of international factors which have considerably reduced the leverage that African rulers can exercise on their former 'patrons'.

The present international political agenda is dominated by the twin imperatives of economic liberalization and democratization, the two being in practice intimately connected. Indeed, there are now clear, if usually covert, political conditionalities to the granting of aid by the Bretton Woods institutions. And most donor countries have either made their bilateral aid dependent on meeting the World Bank conditions or redirected their foreign aid through multilateral rather than bilateral channels. The net effect of these cumulative changes is that the political options of African rulers have been greatly curtailed. Although they can still seek to extract aid from those Western countries like France for which the African agenda remains important, they can no longer use international rivalries to the same profitable effect.

Given this situation, then, is it possible that African leaders now seek to negotiate foreign aid in exchange for agreeing to the transition to multi-party political systems which the West demands? This may appear an excessively cynical and jaundiced view of what is called the democratization of Africa. It may also seem to leave little place for the strong domestic movements in favour of democracy currently to be found in many African countries. We cannot, however, ignore the facts as they present themselves to us. Indeed, it would be strange if African rulers should suddenly cease to use the 'politics of the mirror' in order to maximize foreign aid at the very time when the need for it is greatest. It simply cannot be a coincidence that, now that the West ties aid to democratization under the guise of multi-party elections, multi-party elections are taking place in Africa.

On the face of it, present political transitions to multi-party political systems can be seen as a triumph of Western influence in Africa. But this may prove to be an illusion. African rulers might no longer be able to play one set of countries against another as during the Cold War, but they are beginning to negotiate the very threat of disorder and chaos. Foreign aid will henceforth be required to maintain the façade of democracy which multi-party elections in practice are. Failure to continue to provide aid will raise the spectre of discord, violence, or even civil war. The West, already frightened, to use Kaplan's words,[9] by the gathering 'anarchy' in Africa, will find it difficult to resist demands made by seemingly democratic rulers. The alternatives to these admittedly seriously flawed multi-party systems would be civil strife or generalized brutality, as indeed has already occurred in several African countries (Liberia, Somalia, Rwanda, Zaire, etc.), liable to make the continuation of any form of normal economic links with Africa impossible and bringing to the world's screens images of unbearable suffering and cruelty.

However alarming it may be, we must consider seriously the possibility that some African elites are now 'bargaining' very dangerously the all too real threat of disorder, violence and crime for a continuation of the foreign aid on which their very political, if not personal, survival depends. The same goes for the so-called criminalization of Africa, a process whereby African elites increasingly turn to illicit activities in order to obtain the resources which they need. The growth of violence and crime in Africa would thus, in part at least, be a macabre game of international relations played by rulers who have very few obviously 'legitimate' political cards left to play.

How useful is structural adjustment?

Structural adjustment, adopted by virtually all African countries, has obviously been a response by the Bretton Woods institutions to the African economic crisis. Ostensibly, it is meant to impose financial and fiscal order, to scale back state intervention and to encourage exports – in short to reduce state control and promote the free market. In practice, however, it cannot be shown convincingly that structural adjustment has lessened Africa's dependence. Nor, crucially, has it undermined the clientelistic foundations of power in Africa. On the contrary,

---

[9] R.D. Kaplan, 'The Coming Anarchy: how scarcity, crime, overpopulation and disease are rapidly destroying the social fabric of our planet', *Atlantic Monthly*, February 1994.

it could well be argued that it is structural adjustment which has saved the patrimonial African state from complete economic ruin.

Leaving aside the technical arguments about the success of structural adjustment, on which there is little agreement,[10] we want here to examine the reasons why it has failed to achieve its 'political' aims, that is, to reduce the state's patrimonial and predatory capacity. Is it because foreign aid continues to be channelled through the state? Is it because the state exercises excessive control over the marketing of export crops and manipulates internal pricing as well as the value of the currency? Or is it because of the nature of the links between state and society that we discussed in Part I of this book? Our analysis is in three parts: we look first at the economic impact of structural adjustment; we then discuss its political implications; we end with a consideration of the ways in which African rulers have managed to domesticate structural adjustment.

(a) The economics of structural adjustment. The origins of structural adjustment lie in the diagnosis that the economic policies of most African governments were not viable, in part at least because the state had prevented the market from functioning effectively. Above and beyond the measures intended to restore basic financial and budgetary balances, structural adjustment concentrated on the need to liberalize the economy, free the market, facilitate investment, adjust the currency to realistic exchange levels, control inflation, reduce state expenditures and promote the export of products in which the country had a 'comparative advantage'. In short, African governments were to reduce state profligacy and interference with the market, both internal and international.

Although many of these measures made good economic sense, since many African countries were massively indebted if not bankrupt, their cumulative effect was often damaging. They led to cutbacks in state personnel and the bureaucracy. They implied severe reduction, or complete elimination, of subsidies on basic commodities. They brought about drastic reductions in state expenditures in such important areas as education, health and basic social infrastructure. The immediate consequence of these changes was to weaken the already precarious situation of a very large number of Africans and often resulted in social unrest or even protest against government policies.

The theory of structural adjustment held that in the long run the efflorescence of the market, in all its many private sector activities, would spur economic growth. However, in the short term there

---

[10] See here, for example, Finn Tarp, *Stabilization and Structural Adjustment* (London: Routledge, 1993) and Tony Killick, *IMF Programmes in Developing Countries* (London: Routledge, 1995).

seemed little reward for the strictures imposed by the World Bank. At best, economic reforms brought about a tightening of government expenditures and a cleaning up of state accounting procedures. The liberalization of the economy, for its part, did not deliver on its promises: the benefits of the expansion of the market did not make up for the impact on the population of the sharp cuts in government spending on social and economic activities. Urban dwellers, in particular, suffered higher levels of unemployment and a serious fall in their standards of living.

Such has been the critique of structural adjustment that the World Bank has now begun to rethink a position that was always driven by questionable assumptions about the dynamics of economic development. It has now been acknowledged that the social impact of structural adjustment was both unacceptable and counter-productive, even from the strict economic standpoint. It has also been recognized that, left to its own devices, the market will not bring about serious economic growth in Africa: indeed, open borders and the export of primary products have not led to sustained development anywhere in the world. Moreover, privatization has enabled highly dubious practices, favouring state elites, which are inimical to development as understood by the Bretton Woods institutions. Finally, and crucially, the World Bank has completely revised its position on the putative function of the state in Africa, admitting belatedly that the state had played a crucial role in all those (mostly Asian) countries which have achieved sustained economic development in the recent past.[11]

(b) The politics of structural adjustment. Indeed, the intended, if at times covert, political aim of structural adjustment has been to weaken the state, seen in the 1980s as the chief impediment to economic growth. Starting from the accurate, if superficial, observation that the state was both ubiquitous and predatory, the Bretton Woods institutions conceived the notion that development in Africa was primarily hampered by the weight, inefficiency and corruption of the state. Nevertheless, the very nature of structural adjustment was itself contradictory: the adjustment reforms were to be implemented by the very state which was intended to be 'reduced'. Furthermore, the reward for adjustment was renewed financial aid to the state.

Given the patrimonial nature of the state in Africa and given its role as the main economic actor, structural adjustment posed a real challenge to African rulers. On the one hand, they had to comply with the measures imposed, thereby reducing considerably their ability to nourish their clientelistic networks. Moreover, they had to face the

[11] See World Bank, *World Development Report 1997: the state in a changing world* (Washington, DC: World Bank, 1997).

wrath of the population suffering from the austerity measures imposed by adjustment. The most immediate political danger to those rulers was the possibility that disaffected clients with networks of their own would tap popular discontent and defy the regime. Thus it was that, in both Zambia and Tanzania, the government refused on some occasions to implement, or even reversed, some of the adjustment measures. In a very real sense, therefore, the effects of structural adjustment were politically destabilizing.

At the same time, failure to comply with World Bank and IMF demands meant that most foreign aid was cut off, since by the 1980s Western donors tied aid to compliance with structural adjustment. This interruption in external funding was unsustainable for most African regimes, even if they retaliated by suspending their (in most cases very meagre) debt repayments, since in many cases governments depended on it for recurrent expenditures and the purchase of food. The suspension of aid removed at a stroke much of the resource base of political patrons, thus threatening fatally to weaken their position. It was, therefore, inevitable that, with very few exceptions, all African regimes would in the end comply with structural adjustment. Their only realistic option in this respect was to delay the implementation of adjustment and undermine its effects in other, more subterranean, ways.

(c) The taming of structural adjustment. The failure of structural adjustment programmes to induce sustainable growth, let alone development, in any African country (including such success stories as Ghana) raises the question of whether the schemes are inherently flawed or whether they are simply not workable in the African context. More generally, can economic and political conditionalities really achieve structural changes in present African societies? We shall not here enter the debate about the strictly economic merits of structural adjustment – a controversial topic which would require a quite separate analysis[12] – but focus instead on the ways in which African rulers have succeeded in preventing structural adjustment from undermining the patrimonial and prebendal foundations of the state.

Although in the initial stages of the structural adjustment reforms, governments in Africa were often weakened and destabilized, at least on the surface, most African rulers have since managed to adjust to adjustment. It is true that the combined effects of structural adjustment and multi-party elections have led to the demise of a number of politicians, but some have now re-emerged and most are still active (as

---

[12] For a sharply delineated case study of the economic demerit of structural adjustment see Joseph Hanlon, *Peace without Profit: how the IMF blocks rebuilding in Mozambique* (Oxford: James Currey, 1996).

explained in Chapter 3). They have not, however, fundamentally altered the way in which politics works in contemporary Black Africa. This is primarily because African rulers, far from being interested in using structural adjustment to induce more sustained economic growth, are in fact more concerned to employ the foreign aid thus made available for the selfsame patrimonial purposes.

Structural adjustment has, we believe, been instrumentalized politically with quite some success in two important ways. It has provided the African elites with a new external cause, or scapegoat, for the economic crisis which their countries suffer. Whereas previously failures were attributed in turn to the legacy of colonial rule, to neo-colonialism, imperialism and neo-imperialism, today it is the demands and constraints imposed by the World Bank and the IMF which are presented as the chief reasons for the harsh economic environment in which most Africans have to live. African rulers argue, and argue plausibly, that such austerity is the price their country is forced to pay to the West in order to get the foreign aid it needs. They neglect to point out that the reforms imposed by structural adjustment, many of which were in any event necessary, can now be put in place without facing in full the consequences of the austerity which they demand.

On the other hand, structural adjustment is a blessing in disguise for African rulers for it provides them with the means by which to extract a level of foreign aid which otherwise would not be available to them. As states seemingly follow the edicts of the IMF and the World Bank, these institutions acquire over time a vested interest in seeing the structural adjustment experiment succeed. Despite the realization that African governments have very largely managed to overcome the consequences of adjustment without having implemented the economic reforms which it entails, the West is reluctant to stop aid to those countries which appear to comply. In effect, then, structural adjustment has been 'Africanized' – that is, adapted to the realities of the patrimonial system. The Bretton Woods institutions are themselves having to reconsider the purposes of adjustment since the option of cutting off foreign aid to African states is not realistic, if only because of the fear of disorder, violence and crime which it might bring about.[13]

If this is indeed what is happening in Africa, then the failure of structural adjustment would have less to do with the defects of the schemes *per se* – although these are many – than with its successful political instrumentalization by the African elites. This, in turn, raises the question of how Africans can 'develop' in the sense in which it is usually understood in the West.

---

[13] And what happened to the United Nations in Somalia is now seared into the consciousness of the main Western countries.

9

The (In)significance of Development

There appears to be a general impression, which we believe to be misleading, that Africa is on the 'threshold of development', as though it were merely a matter of a little more effort before the continent achieves sustainable economic growth and political institutionalization. This presumption seems in the end to be shared by both liberal and neo-Marxist analysts. The former see the present situation as a crisis of adaptation: Africa is making the painful transition to modernity. The latter see the continuation of neo-colonial relations as the main reason for the delayed progress of the continent. Above and beyond their diverging ideologies, however, development for advocates of both sides is only a matter of time and will-power.

Several decades after Africa's independences, and in the face of the present economic crisis, it seems reasonable to ask whether one ought not to consider another approach. As it becomes clear to Africans and Africanists alike that, whatever the reasons adduced for the absence of progress, very little development has in fact been achieved, the question of causality grows ever more insistent. What is holding Africa back? Why is there so little evidence that African governments are implementing the development policies to which they claim to be committed? What would make it possible for the continent to 'take off'?

In the face of such persistent questions, we believe it is time to examine whether the endurance of a certain number of key societal characteristics is inimical to the in-depth change of the continent which development as we know it would demand. We are aware that this is indeed a controversial area. However, it is interesting and chastening to note that, despite the weight of the current political correctness which has had such a deadening impact on African studies, a number of African authors are beginning to move off the beaten interpretative track and suggest more realistic culture-based explanations.

Following on from what we have outlined so far in this book, we propose to go beyond current justifications for the absence of economic progress and suggest that, contrary to what has hitherto been assumed, development as we conceive it might in effect not be *the* priority for a majority of Africans. Indeed, we need to look beyond the most immediate and perhaps most superficial level of what is being discussed formally by state officials and donor partners. If we study, empirically, what is happening in most African countries, we believe it is reasonable to ask whether the continent is not following a different agenda. It is, in fact, quite possible that this part of the world is heading in a distinct, decidedly non-Western, direction: modernity without development. This might well mean that Africa, though economically marginalized, is still capable of playing its part in the world of international exchange: globalization in the opposite direction, as it were. It is to this perplexing question that we devote this chapter.

Non-development: reasons and rationale

There has probably been more written on issues of development than on any other topic and it is not our intention here to review this literature. The complexity of the historical process has prompted economists, political scientists, anthropologists, sociologists and other 'experts' to propound a multitude of hypotheses and to formulate countless proposals for change, all of which are in some way or other based on the experiences or expectations of the West. Given the obvious failures of many of the imported schemes, a number of Africanists have, in turn, offered 'indigenous' designs for development, supposedly more in keeping with the values of the societies concerned. For them, modernization would no longer result from the laborious adaptation of foreign models but would be based on the continent's 'genius', in continuity with its own civilization. Here, however, one is prompted to ask what precisely such an autochthonous model would imply, since to this day there have been no realistic proposals for practicable indigenous development plans. More recently, no doubt because of the severity of the current economic crisis and the need for Western succour, there has arisen a resigned or instrumental acceptance of the so-called tried and tested liberal solutions on which aid donors insist.

Nevertheless, what is remarkable is that, despite the continued failure of development on the continent, there has been scarcely any serious discussion of the relevance of the concept, other than in relatively technical terms. It is, of course, not difficult to understand why the aspiration to develop remains symbolically 'sacred', for Africans as well as for outsiders: it has to do with national self-respect, with the need for African elites to acquire an internationally respectable political legitimacy and with the obligation for all to project a viable future for Africa. Yet what this means is that there appears to be a compulsion for ideological voluntarism continuously to override any analytical disillusionment or doubt. To many Africanists, the present crisis remains merely the prelude to a better tomorrow.

There is widespread abuse of the metaphor of the 'bitter medicine' which will hasten the 'recovery' of the continent. Even in the face of the most relentlessly dismal statistics on the absence of growth in Africa, there is ever-renewed insistence on Africa's potential, its underestimated dynamism and inventiveness. One cannot help but conclude that the optimism of such inveterate redeemers of the continent, however well-meaning, draws on blind faith in *a priori* concepts of economic development. Is it not time, therefore, that we give consideration to the possibility that such notions of development always have been, and may well continue to be, quite misleading?

Existing interpretations suffer from one of two congenital defects: illusive universalism or excessive economic dogma. Following the independence of most African countries in the 1960s, and within the context of the ideological rivalry engendered by the Cold War, the early years of development theory involved an extremely mechanical transposition of concepts fashioned in respect of very distinct Western or Eastern settings. During at least two decades, so-called experts merely transferred their blueprints to an environment whose historical, social and cultural specificities they hardly knew, or even cared to discover.

On the liberal side, the notion prevailed that only the West possessed both the conceptual know-how and the technical wherewithal to promote the development of a continent which was in such dire need of their assistance. For the opposite side, the emphasis was to be placed on Africa's deteriorating terms of trade, its growing indebtedness, or the pillage of its resources, all jeopardizing its future progress. Salvation was seen to lie in the creation of an independent industrial base protected from the capitalist greed of the 'multinational ogres'. Beyond their different credos, however, both sides shared a common messianic approach. Their respective iron laws of development were claimed to be as universally valid as the theory of gravitation. Thus, Africa's poor performance came to be explained either in terms of temporary dysfunctions or imperialist exploitation.

Subsequently, a new generation of more empirically based analysts brought a greater critical perspective to the study of development in Africa. Doubts were raised about the value of existing statistics, the types of indicators used and, above all, about the assumptions made in respect of the dynamic of economic growth. Furthermore, what could be observed on the ground proved to be a challenge to the conceptual supremacy of the political economy approach. A number of

Africanists, many of them anthropologists, began to point out the degree to which the development paradigms used rested on Western-based concepts of markets, productive accumulation or class formation that hardly made sense in the African context.

For years Western intellectuals, disillusioned by the experience of their own countries, had believed they could simply transfer their 'revolutionary' fervour and apply their analytical categories to Africa. Empirical research now showed that Marxist or 'developmentalist' concepts failed to account for what was happening south of the Sahara, where politics evidently continued to function within the prevailing framework of informal, familial and clientelistic networks. Such fieldwork demonstrated that the socio-political realities of the continent were distinct from those assumed by theories of Western- or Eastern-based modernization. This reversal of perspective on the notion of development in Africa has rendered obsolete a wide range of approaches, although a number of current interpretative disagreements continue to rest on defunct ideological or disciplinary disputes.[1]

The publication in recent years of several original and provocative essays written by Africans themselves marks a turning point in the discussion of the possible causes for the absence of development on the continent. Their implacably critical view of what has happened south of the Sahara is interesting for several important reasons. There is here for the first time an attempt to understand the *internal* (as opposed to the commonly cited external) grounds for the present state of affairs. A Cameroonian writes incisively about the 'myth of the African will for development', that all too often is a way of obscuring local incompetence by reference to the so-called international neo-colonial plot.[2]

The author cannot find words strong enough to berate African hypocrisy, inertia and ideological complacency. She writes: '[one] cannot but be struck by the deliberate manner in which Africans refuse any rational approach to organisation [...] At all levels, there is systematic recourse to improvisation, tinkering and approximation.' She refers to 'a deadly conformism', 'unacceptable signs of backwardness', as well as 'a complete lack of a critical stance in respect of local values', and she does not hesitate to use the notion of 'underdevelopment' (for Africa).[3] Elsewhere, she writes that 'it is indeed striking how back-

---

[1] For an interesting example of such debates a decade ago, that is revealing about both the French and the Anglo-Saxon approaches, see *Politique Africaine*, 26 (June 1987) on 'Classes, Etat, Marchés', published soon after the release of Richard Sandbrook (with Judith Barker), *The Politics of Africa's Political Stagnation* (Cambridge: Cambridge University Press, 1985), and more particularly Jean Copans' remarks in the Introduction to the dossier on the conceptual crisis.

[2] Kabou, 1991, 18 and 29.

[3] *Ibid.*, pp. 23, 25, 26, 38.

ward attitudes, considered unacceptable elsewhere in the world, continue to prevail at all levels of society in Africa, thus making worse an already precarious situation and preventing much needed changes'.[4]

Kabou thus touches on a number of what we, for our part, believe to be key issues. She acknowledges that certain failings affect all layers of society, from top to bottom. She is clear that the situation in Africa is worsening but that, at the same time, there is a great reluctance to introduce the necessary in-depth reforms. Undoubtedly this virulent and somewhat voluntarist approach to Africa's predicament remains problematic from the analytical perspective, as we shall discuss below. Nevertheless, it is interesting to note how her conclusions about the current African predicament are entirely consistent with our interpretation of the significance of the process of informalization and the reluctance to institutionalize.

What is noteworthy is the importance given by these African authors to cultural features as determinants of development. They focus attention upon the need for an analysis based on the study of mentalities.[5] Another Cameroonian writer asks, with a pleasantly mischievous sense of humour, whether Africa does not in reality need 'a *cultural* adjustment programme'.[6] For this author, the fundamental reason why the continent south of the Sahara has 'deviated' from the common developmental norm is 'African culture', the 'common core' of which includes: apathy, a large dose of fatalism, a peculiar relation to the notion of time, the insignificance of the individual in the face of the community, a tendency to 'convivial' excesses, the primacy of conflict avoidance and the weight of the 'irrational'.[7]

It could be argued, not without reason, that such generalizations are no more than clichés, but as we all know stereotypes can often be revealing. Two ideas seem to us interesting in Manguele's book. The first is that the author argues that the artificial maintenance of consensus in Africa is counter-productive. The second is that he advocates the urgent institutionalization of the resolution of social conflicts on the continent. If his verdict – adapt or die – is a little extreme, it is notable that he refers to the Braudelian lesson of the benefits of learning from other civilizations.[8] His conclusion is thus a far cry from the perennial clamour for a singular 'African way', since it is in essence a

---

[4] *Ibid.*, pp. 12–13.
[5] 'There are no politicians arising out of nothing, no societies without mentalities'. *Ibid.*, p. 12.
[6] Daniel Etounga-Manguele, *L'Afrique a-t-elle besoin d'un programme d'ajustement culturel?* (Ivry: Editions nouvelles du Sud, 1991).
[7] *Ibid.*, pp. 34ff.
[8] *Ibid.*, pp. 86ff.

call for the continent's inhabitants to reform and adopt those methods which have proved successful in other parts of the world.[9]

A Senegalese economist, M. L. Diallo, also reflects on 'the main tendencies of the African psychology'.[10] If Etounga-Manguele's essay stressed the 'non-productivity of African capital' and 'the lack of motivation', Diallo emphasizes the continent's inability to move beyond an economy of exchange. He insists on the profound ambiguities of the 'rentier mode of production', which does not involve the extraction of surplus from the lower classes by the higher classes but consists instead in the acquisition of resources outside the country for redistribution inside.[11] Diallo also stresses the absence of the notion of individual merit in Africa, social success being generally explained within a collective perspective, involving at times reference to the use of the occult. The author thus believes that the African reputation for 'laziness' is the consequence of two main factors: the lack of any intrinsic value attached to work and a notion of prosperity that is unrelated to diligence.

Clearly, what is new in such arguments is a self-critical approach rejecting the habitual exculpating explanations of Africa's predicament and focusing attention both on the putative incompatibility of African culture(s) with modern economic development and on the hitherto virtually taboo question of mentalities. For decades, it was virtually unacceptable seriously to consider such issues since they would almost inevitably have been regarded as the remnants of an imperial outlook or even racist prejudices.[12] After all, under colonial rule, cultural differences were readily employed as instruments of domination, of contempt – hence the understandable tendency to reject an emphasis on such factors as facile xenophobia. Unfortunately, those well-meaning responses eventually brought about a stifling political correctness, an excess of analytical conformism which all too readily branded as racist any attempt to discuss these issues, an attitude that eventually hampered our understanding of the continent. It ought now to be possible to give attention to cultural factors without giving the slightest credence to those who believe in the innate inferiority of Africans.[13]

[9] See here also Jean-Baptiste Onana, 'De la relation entre culture et développement: leçons asiatiques pour l'Afrique', *Politique Africaine*, 68 (December 1997).

[10] Mamadou Lamine Diallo, *Les Africains sauveront-ils l'Afrique?* (Paris: Karthala, 1996), p. 26.

[11] For more details on this argument see *ibid.*, pp. 30ff.

[12] On the lines of the infamous Rhodesian saying: 'You can take the African out of the bush but you cannot take the bush out of the African'!

[13] An absurd position which can easily be dismissed on the very simple ground that a large number of Africans have shown that, given the right circumstances, they can excel in their own field of endeavour.

Furthermore, our argument is not that Africa's lack of development is solely to be explained in cultural terms. Quite obviously, the global economic constraints of the world market outlined by dependency theorists have had a crippling effect on the continent's potential for growth.[14] Nevertheless, we would contend that it is impossible to explain the current economic crisis south of the Sahara without taking into account cultural factors. This does not in any way mean that we favour the popular view that Africa would in some (mysterious) way be stuck in an immutable and timeless rut, a defect found in some of the economists we have mentioned. We are merely emphasizing how important it is to recognize how little work has been done on the question of culture. This is all the more surprising since such research has proved invaluable, most notably for the French historians of *'mentalités'*, whose publications have shed so much light on how the evolution of cultural representations affects social behaviour.

Regrettably, the discussion of cultural ruptures and continuities is all too frequently cast in simplistic dichotomies: prejudged ideas on the unchanging or dynamic character of Africa in this respect. We are not persuaded by arguments in favour of either a 'timeless' Africa, whose apparent transformation would be mere artifice, or of the huge potential for change exhibited by the region. What we want to understand more concretely is the cultural matrix within which Africa's own distinct modernization is taking place. Instead of pillorying the continent's 'backwardness', as the authors cited above largely do, we think it more profitable to analyse the anthropological evidence for existing, and clearly enduring, mentalities which are relevant to the politics of Africa. Of these we would stress fatalism, understood as a rational response to the huge degree of uncertainty faced by most of the continent's population, and the primacy of the collective over the individual, itself the outcome of a realistic appraisal of what constitutes the best guarantee of survival in the face of a perennially threatening outside world.[15] The major problem in the discussion of such issues is that it seems difficult to move away from teleological approaches.

It would undoubtedly be instructive to undertake a sociological study of those African intellectuals, like the authors cited above, educated in the most prestigious Western universities and much influenced by their experience within international institutions such as the United Nations, World Bank and the IMF. Their tendency to be both critical and pre-

---

[14] What we reject is the dependency theorists' insistence on external factors as the *ultima ratio* of, if not the sole reason for, the continent's failure to develop.

[15] In this respect, there is merit in re-examining the conclusions of such an unfashionable anthropologist as Lucien Lévy-Bruhl, particularly with regard to his remarks about the African capacity to accommodate contradictions regardless of behavioural coherence, an ability which is fast disappearing in the Western world.

scriptive evokes that of the clever students keen to teach their less bright colleagues what they have just learnt. Their self-awareness is naturally encouraging, demonstrating as it does legitimate concerns about the economic stagnation and marginalization of Africa. Nevertheless, their excess of what seems a very Western type of voluntarism may not augur well for the implementation of their admittedly well thought-out and often entirely appropriate remedies for the continent. In addition, there is evidence that such intellectuals not infrequently fail to live up to their own standards when they return to Africa, adjusting all too readily (like Soglo, Benin's first democratically elected president) to the cultural norms they had previously so sternly criticized.

Given the conclusions of our previous chapters, we wonder whether the continued dominance of the informalization of politics in sub-Saharan Africa is compatible with sustained economic growth. Indeed, development would require the channelling of immense energy and resources by means of co-ordinated, institutionalized political and economic entities operating above existing particularistic dynamics. As Weber already noted long ago, the minimal conditions of predictability and judicial protection, which are the building blocks of a modern economy, are incompatible with a patrimonial system. This is without a doubt the heart of the problem on the continent. For us, however, it is less important to find out whether Africa 'refuses to develop', whether it needs 'a cultural adjustment programme', or whether 'it will be saved by Africans', than to ascertain whether it is following a relatively rational road to modernity, however unpalatable some of its characteristics may appear to be.

Is development a priority?

Even if we see the merit of the arguments offered by the African analysts cited above, we do not subscribe to their implicit or explicit notion that all that is required to overcome Africa's natural 'torpor'[16] is a leap forward – and this for several reasons. First, our ambitions are not normative: we have no intention of offering prescriptions from the outside. Second, we believe that such injunctions are likely to turn out to be nothing other than wishful thinking: development cannot merely be decreed from above, especially where the appropriate political institutions are not functioning.

Finally, as we have explained repeatedly, our approach to culture is not just an allusion to given 'values' but refers to a general framework,

---

[16] To borrow an expression used by Célestin Monga as cited by Etounga-Manguele, *op. cit.*, p.12.

a matrix, which, however constraining, is liable to change over time. We reject the facile explanations based on a vision of a timeless Africa, but because of this we are all the more mindful of the need to ground our analysis in the *'longue durée'*. Our view of the enduring force of certain cultural characteristics on the continent rests on an interpretation of their instrumental significance, rather than simply on the weight of Africa's inertia.

What are these characteristics and how do they matter? They derive quite naturally from the material we have presented in the previous chapters. Among the most significant factors for our analysis we would highlight the following: the inability or unwillingness to institutionalize more formal and impersonal social relations; the reluctance to accept a Western socio-economic and political order, despite repeated commitments to that effect; and, finally, the subtle use of distinct registers of socio-political behaviour that may well not be compatible (at least seen from the perspective of our own Western rationality).

We stress three points. The first is that the African post-colonial cultural order we have described throughout the book constitutes a distinct universe, the understanding of which helps to account for the events and processes with which we are here concerned. What we observe in Africa is not a resort to 'imagined' or frozen cultural customs, used purposefully to 'assert one's difference'.[17] It is a spontaneous and rational recourse to a deeply rooted cultural environment. Second, this mindset is shared by all layers of the population and it would be deceptive as well as hypocritical to argue that it does not apply to the elites. We reject, therefore, those interpretations favouring the view that such cultural beliefs are manipulated for ideological motives, and argue instead that there is a shared 'heritage' valid for all and which all can aspire to use instrumentally.

Third, we would maintain that, given the current norms of political rationality throughout the world, this perennial preference in Africa for the infra-institutional is best understood from the standpoint of disorder. Nevertheless, it is also possible to interpret the primacy of the informal as deriving from a different logic and resulting in a distinct type of modernity which goes against the grain of most existing models. It is thus crucial to modulate our perspective according to the focus of analysis. At the macro-sociological level, what is occurring in Africa is the negation of the Western type of development. As far as (political) actors are concerned, however, this type of behaviour may well turn out to be most eminently rational. In other, plainer, words it

---

[17] A thesis put forward by Claude Meillassoux which we would reject. See his 'Consommer la rupture', in Marc Piault, *La colonisation: rupture ou parenthèse* (Paris; L'Harmattan, 1987), p. 54.

is possible for a country's economy to fall into ruin, for development to be insignificant, while at the same time the members of a large number of (informal) networks continue substantially to enrich themselves. It may even be true that economic failure is in this respect at least more 'profitable' for many than 'development'.

In view of the paradox thus presented, it is essential to remind ourselves that perceptions of self-interest are determined by one's view of the world. We follow here Weber, who maintained that human behaviour was only intelligible within the context of the conception which individuals had of their existence. For this reason, our position stands clear of what we believe to be two extreme positions, both leading to interpretative dead ends. There is, on the one hand, a structuralist view according to which Africans behave without proper understanding of the constraints which determine their attitudes. On the other hand, we find a radical anti-culturalist stance, the thrust of which is that the phenomena we describe here can be explained in terms of the strategies of the dominant elites.[18] For us, politicians have a relative autonomy of action within the context of distinctly African cultural environments which are not universal, or banal. Such cultural constraints, however, seem to engender a dynamic of modernization which is decidedly atypical on the eve of the twenty-first century.

Some observers have been concerned about the possibility that Westernization would extinguish the African 'soul'. However, as Kabou says quite rightly: 'whoever has lived, however briefly, in Black Africa (even in the capital city) will immediately be aware how immune the African is to Westernisation'.[19] Others stress more subtly the hybridization of world cultures, although in the case of Africa they might well be misled as to the extent and significance of cultural miscegenation. Some Africans (and not a few Africanists!) hold what appears to be a contradictory position. On the one hand, they deplore that the continent should for ever be seen as exotic and assert the need for a more universalist approach. On the other, they are quick to decry cultural imperialism and defend Africa's singularity in the face of the West's condemnation of many of the continent's practices. For example, well-to-do Beninois families have rejected the accusation of some Western human rights organizations censuring the exploitation of young village girls sent to Cotonou to work as domestic servants, on the grounds that foreigners understand nothing about Africa. Their view is that, within a logic of reciprocity between city and country-

---

[18] Which would appear to be the position held by Jean-François Bayart in *L'illusion identitaire* (Paris: Fayard, 1997), p. 10.

[19] Kabou, *op. cit.*, p. 56.

side, poor village families benefit equally from no longer having to sustain girls who can live in urban centres.

In a now classic article, the anthropologist Emmanuel Terray draws a distinction between the world of the 'air-conditioner' and the world of the 'veranda'.[20] The former pertains to certain hours of the day, certain official settings: its function is less to manage than to show, particularly to the outside, that the country works, that it holds its rank in the concert of nations. The latter, more personalized, more relaxed, stands for a less visible, more subterranean, realm of reciprocity. The metaphor is useful if, as the author stresses, it is not taken to be a simplistic opposition between modernity and tradition. From our viewpoint, a large proportion of Africanist literature has failed to understand the extent to which the formal domain of the 'air-conditioner' was superficial and, conversely, how fundamental that of the 'veranda' continued to be. An interpretation of the African political order based on the apparent institutional similarity with the West must therefore be seen either as uninspired or uninformed, incapable as it is of assessing the insignificance of the symbol of the 'air-conditioner' which comforts both the African elites and the outside world.

This cosy informal arrangement is conveniently practical, and not just for Africans. There are many claims of external complicity. It is commonly alleged that suitcases full of money have regularly been taken from African capitals to Paris on the eve of French elections – all, naturally, in the name of personal bonds of 'friendship'. More pointedly, Francophone African heads of state managed to induce President Mitterrand to sack Jean-Pierre Cot, his Minister for Co-operation, whose moral intransigence (some would say naiveté) disturbed existing working relations. In the normal course of events, it is reported that French diplomats, businessmen and '*coopérants*' are effortlessly persuaded to play their part in illicit activities which serve their interests. In such circumstances, then, who, in the end, is 'contaminating' whom? It is true that Africans are generally fascinated by the modern world. At the same time, however, there are a good number of Westerners who, annoyed at what they see as the excessive regulatory constraints imposed by a strong state in their own countries of origin, consider Africa as one of the last 'free' continents, a region where it is possible to disdain prohibitions without fear of the penalties which apply in the West.

Given this relationship between African and the former colonial powers, when Africanophile writers say that 'we need Africa',[21] we would be tempted to ask for what purpose. Admittedly, a number of

---

[20] Terray, 1986.
[21] Eric Fottorino, Christophe Guillemin, Erik Orsena, *Besoin d'Afrique* (Paris: Fayard, 1992).

observers seem genuinely to fear the increasing marginalization of the continent in the post-Cold War era. They believe there is a risk that the West will forsake some African countries (the case of Somalia being the first example), only intervening where it has direct economic interests or where it dreads large-scale emigration. Nevertheless, fantasies about an exotically fulfilling Africa, perceived as a counterpoint to our own over-stressed and desiccated societies, continue to exercise a hold on our Western imaginations.

One might well ask, therefore, whether Africa's rejection of the classical logic of economic development, and the strengthening political and economic informalization of the continent, do not in fact constitute a comparative advantage. Could African disorder also be instrumentalized at the international level? Is it not at least plausible that the growing international parallel economy would find it convenient to use Africa as its major conduit? Here we share the views of those Africanists currently working on the so-called 'criminalization of the state' when they emphasize that there is on the continent 'a situation of anarchy [...] propitious to the development of informal networks', where 'nothing can be taken for granted because everything is open to parallel negotiation'.[22]

We would argue, however, that our analysis is more finely attuned to African realities. As far as we are concerned, it is inaccurate to speak of 'the privatization of power' or of the 'delegitimation of public services' since it gives the erroneous impression that the state was at some stage properly regulated. There has not been a 'deliquescence' of political processes simply because they were never institutionalized in the first place. The informal has always been predominant in Africa, even if the present crisis brings about a fragmentation of patronage networks whilst the shrinkage of existing resources induces still greater informalization. We do not think, therefore, that it is realistic to suggest that such informal practices will diminish in the foreseeable future or, more crucially, that there is on the continent any aspiration to do away with them.

We would stress instead that Africa is not degenerating, nor is it 'blocked', but that it is forging ahead, following its own path, although assuredly at great variance with existing models of development. Where chaos is overcome, as in Uganda for example, it does not necessarily mean that the country is westernizing. Even when African political leaders appear eager to abide by the rules set by aid donors to qual-

---

[22] Béatrice Hibou, 'Le capital social de l'Etat falsificateur' in Jean-Francois Bayart, Stephen Ellis and Béatrice Hibou, *La criminalisation de l'Etat en Afrique* (Bruxelles: Editions Complexe, 1997) pp. 138–9; translated as *The Criminalization of the State in Africa* (Oxford: James Currey, 1999).

ify for much needed aid, their entourage ensures that they remain aware of the primacy of infra-institutional considerations. More generally, there is serious doubt as to whether it is worthwhile for politicians to try to set up a properly regulated state and to guarantee the rule of law when there is so much to gain for so many from a continuous climate of insecurity. The enormous increase in the number of private security firms, in which former soldiers, policemen or guerrillas find employment, is one small but revealing example of the many ways in which disorder can be usefully instrumentalized.

Equally, we find it instructive that young graduates should be attracted to the position of 'traditional chief' because they see it as more stable than a political or administrative career. This phenomenon of what are called 'newbreed chiefs' in Nigeria shows how fruitful it can be to operate on such traditional registers, even if, as happens, such chieftaincies are created *ex nihilo* in some of the cities' newest quarters. African elites, even when they use their own private jets to go and speculate in the world's major financial centres, remain prey to 'irrational' beliefs long disappeared in the West. The question is whether they cannot, or do not want to, transcend such occult constraints. Conversely, those in Africa who may appear 'traditional' frequently employ the most sophisticated technological equipment, symbolized, as it were, by the ubiquitous satellite dish and the mobile telephone.

The question of the apparent dichotomy between modernity and tradition is not simple. A large number of so-called 'archaic' characteristics currently to be found south of the Sahara were common practices in Europe or North America not so long ago. Nevertheless, and this is the gist of our argument, there is no indication that a similar socio-political and economic evolution will take place in Africa. Comparisons can easily be made over time. A common argument is that the continent cannot be expected to achieve in a few decades what took Europe and North America centuries. But such reasoning is misleading in so far as the contexts within which different parts of the world develop are radically different. The Industrial Revolution led to an acceleration of economic, social and political change which was even more fundamental than the technological advances it made possible. Similarly, today, we live in a truly globalized world in which models are easily transmitted across borders.

Nevertheless, even within such a context, Africa does not in any way appear to be developing according to any of the existing colonial or postcolonial blueprints. To be fair, full-scale Westernization would require at the very least a gigantic (financial and cultural) investment on the part of the North, which in the present international circumstances is hardly realistic. Nor is there any evidence that such an injection of resources would have the desired effect. Is it, therefore, plausible to expect Africa to follow a given model of development? It is difficult to believe that today the continent's governments will readily heed foreign injunctions and implement the recommendations proffered by the Bretton Woods institutions and other external aid donors. In reality, the best the West can hope for is to negotiate a diplomatically judicious use of co-operation agreements.

The question of whether the Western model of development is either inevitable or even desirable is a matter of conviction which we do not intend to debate here. What we can say, however, is that there are strong indications that the graft of this model on to Africa appears to be rejected, as though in its present form it remained too 'foreign' a body. European modernization was constructed on the ruins of its *anciens régimes*. Is it not at the very least possible that Africa too will do the same? Whatever the case, historians can only register the continent's formidable cultural resistance, its ferocious reluctance to jettison its own socio-political foundations, whether it be through the Africanization of Western norms or by means of an uneasy conflation of the practices promulgated by the North's aid donors with the prevalent values of the continent.

Where, we believe, our argument is original is in suggesting that the present situation in Africa may well be more durable than is generally envisaged. Indeed, the current crisis is likely to reinforce the existing tendencies that we have analysed above. It is, therefore, entirely possible that the continent's economic outlook will remain unconventional: an economy of exchange (barter, even), rather than the more orthodox economy of accumulation, investment, transformation and production predicted by Western theories of economic development. Similarly, Africans may well stay resolutely inimical to the growth of an atomized, individualistic, mass society where solidarity counts for little. Consequently, it is conceivable that the continuation of such communal links will prevent the emergence of individual citizenship, as it will the construction of an institutionalized state.

This, in any case, is what has happened to date on the continent. The export revenues (of agricultural produce or mineral resources) have lubricated the vertical and personalized networks of redistribution which sustain patrimonial relations. What, in the context of an acute economic and financial crisis as well as a growing population, can Africa's prospects now be other than bleak? Although we are in no position to provide more useful forecasts than anyone else, we are impressed by the continent's extraordinary capacity to face up to its problems and survive.

It is appropriate at this stage to return to the notion of modernization. However unorthodox Africa's evolution may appear to be, we must give the fullest consideration to the complex ways in which it has adapted to the realities of the contemporary world. On the one hand, African societies have succeeded in instrumentalizing to good effect the formal Western order they seemingly embrace, as we have shown in respect of the state, civil society, corruption or structural adjustment. On the other, they have continued to evolve, accommodating their belief systems and practices as they see fit to the challenges of Western modernity and globalization.

The primacy of communitarian and clientelistic imperatives leads assuredly to massive economic inefficiency, and possibly to terminal damage at the macro-sociological level: it seems unlikely, for instance, that the health system of most African countries will ever be satisfactory. Yet it is vital to avoid falling prey either to the optimistic economic prognosis currently mooted by the World Bank or to an admittedly more common gloom of 'Afro-pessimism'. The future of the continent may be equivocal but it does not appear to lie in the lessening of informalization. On the contrary, we are likely to witness an increase in informal practices, both domestically and internationally.

IV

A New Paradigm

10
The Political Instrumentalization of Disorder

The quest for an understanding of contemporary Black Africa can often appear elusive, blending as it does a large dose of immediately powerful images of a continent in crisis with a perplexing set of conceptually diverse approaches. That it should be so is not entirely surprising since Africa has, at least from the nineteenth century, been at the centre of the Western imagination of the 'other'. Indeed, it would be interesting, and not a little revealing, to revisit our notion of the continent on the model of Edward Said's well-known study of Orientalism.[1] It would undoubtedly provide a necessary preparation for any well-grounded attempt to explain what it is that we (Western) Africanists do when we try to interpret events in Africa today.[2]

What such a reflection of Africanism would show is that our approach to the continent has been driven by a need to fit its supposed complexities – its enigmatic psychology, as it were – into an explanatory scheme congruent with our view of Western development. Seen from that perspective, Africa has often seemed to represent either the initial stage in our notion of progress or the dark opposite of what Western civilization is taken to represent. Africa has always been – and most obviously continues to be – the backward or the barbarous continent. In other words, Africa's 'otherness' appears systematically to have generated interpretations which are in some very direct sense either normative or teleological.

Leaving aside an examination of the cultural grounds for the Western view of the continent, however enlightening it would be, what is clear is that such perceptions have had a profound influence on the approaches employed to analyse present-day Africa. It is appro-

[1] Edward Said, *Orientalism* (London: Routledge & Kegan Paul, 1978).
[2] For an extended consideration of this question, see Chabal, 1997.

priate to remind ourselves at this juncture that the dominant Africanist social science until the end of colonial rule was anthropology. Indeed, the very discipline of modern social anthropology derived in part from an attempt to answer the grand nineteenth-century questions on human evolution.

There is undoubtedly a parallel here between anthropology and political science since in both instances the spur to conceptualization originated from the need to understand the reasons for radical differences in 'development'. As is well known, the modern discipline of political science was born in the US in the 1950s on the eve of the decolonization of Africa. Not surprisingly, therefore, political scientists were eager to test their fresh theory of political development on the 'virgin' territory of the newly independent countries. Ignorant as they were of African or even colonial history, they contrived to believe that the study of the political evolution of the 'new' African countries would both validate their conceptual framework and advance our understanding of the politics of the continent.

Our intention is not to review the merits of theories of political development but to show how most current paradigms of African politics share common assumptions about the meaning of development.[3] Here explanations have ranged from straightforward Marxist or neo-Marxist interpretations, sundry theories of dependency, to a whole body of political analysis devoted to the examination of the impediments to political institutionalization as occurred in the Western experience. They have all, however, sought to explain why it is that Africa has hitherto failed to develop either along the Western or the Eastern (socialist) models – that is, effectively to modernize. Hence, development is most often used as a codeword for modernization.

The consequences of such an approach are many but we should like to stress two. The first is that historically unrealistic expectations have been generated in terms of the development potential of a modern independent Africa. From that viewpoint, the results are grim, as Africa has not only failed to live up to those expectations but appears 'incomprehensibly' to un-develop. The second, and analytically more significant, is the way in which conceptualization has been tied to a notion of development that implies a purposeful (economic, social and political) historical movement in a given direction. In effect, virtually all models of African politics are constructed on the assumption that development and modernization are coterminous.

[3] For a systematic discussion, see Chabal, 1992, Part I, where the following paradigms are reviewed: development theory, class theory, underdevelopment theory, revolutionary theory and democratic theory.

Such paradigms seek to identify the motor of development: that is, how economic, political and social dynamics might link up causally to make the continent progress. Although it is not in principle unreasonable to attempt to determine the conditions under which Africa would modernize, it is our contention that the practical result of such an approach has been detrimental to our understanding of the continent. This is because it is most difficult, if not impossible, simultaneously to examine the extent to which available data confirm a given theory and to keep an open mind about possible interpretations of what is actually happening on the ground. It might, of course, be argued that such paradigms ought to have been derived from the examination of existing conditions in the first place. But since, as we have pointed out, most paradigms are in fact drawn from the Western (or Eastern socialist) experience, the problem remains acute.

The argument outlined in *Power in Africa* (Chabal, 1992) showed how it is possible to construct a political interpretation of contemporary Africa on the basis of a number of 'universal' concepts of political analysis which are not linked to particular theories. Our ambition in this book has been to provide the building blocks of a paradigm which is both derived from an empirical examination of contemporary African politics and framed conceptually by an approach built on the foundations of what we take to be classical political analysis. What this means concretely is that we have developed a model driven by the realities of what we observe in Africa today but grounded in the social and political theory which underpins the analysis of all modern societies, our own included. We hope in this way to offer both a much sharper understanding of present-day politics in Africa and a more plausible framework for comparing Africa's evolution with that of the rest of the world.

Our paradigm – the political instrumentalization of disorder – is distinct in that it attempts to show how the political, social and economic 'logics' of contemporary Africa come together in a process of modernization which does not fit with the Western experience of development. Our starting point is that Africa's present condition represents a form of singular 'modernization' which needs to be explained. It is not simply that the continent is behind, or backward, or delayed in its development.[4] Our analysis endeavours to explain why Africa is moving in a direction which is not just different from Westernization but

---

[4] This is not to deny that Africa has failed to modernize in the sense in which theories of development had anticipated, nor to deny that it is in crisis, but merely to point out that an explanation for such 'failure' requires a different approach.

also difficult to comprehend by means of existing paradigms. For us, however, the problem in making sense of this singular evolution is not that it is inherently impossible to grasp, but that existing interpretative frameworks are simply too coarse.

Africa, then, is developing differently. Yet the only way to understand the nature of this particular dynamic is to use a universal conceptual apparatus – that is, one constructed according to clear analytical categories congruent with post-Weberian social and political theory. We use such a paradigm to examine the logic of African politics from the local viewpoint: why are Africans acting as they do? Our aim is to go beyond the two most common approaches currently in vogue. The first turns on a variant of the image of Africa as a traditional, unchanging or timeless continent, incapable of adapting to modernity. The second rests on what amounts to paternalism in that it systematically exculpates Africans for their (mis)deeds on the grounds that the continent's present predicament is the result of uncontrollable external forces.

We hope in this way to show how a scientifically grounded approach is compatible with what we would call analytical empathy – that is, the capacity to explain what makes sense to Africans in conceptually rational terms. That is why our paradigm differs significantly from the two dominant schools of thought. The first might be termed Eurocentric in that it takes for granted the validity of what are self-evidently historically determined Western concepts such as development, corruption, civil society or even the state. The other interprets Africa's politics on the basis of generalized, or catch-all, 'African' causalities by way of metaphorical notions such as, for instance, 'the politics of the belly'.[5]

The question of modernity

The chief challenge facing the analyst of contemporary Africa is to explain how the continent can be both modern and undeveloped – that is, what modernization might mean in a context where there is no development as it is normally understood in the West. What we observe in Africa is paradoxical from this point of view: nowhere is the juxtaposition of the obviously 'traditional' with the patently 'modern' more striking. Africans are not slow in adopting the latest technological aids – be they computers or mobile phones – but at the same time

[5] Jean-François Bayart, *The State in Africa: the politics of the belly* (London: Longman, 1993).

they seem locked into apparently 'backward' social or psychological conventions, such as polygamy or witchcraft.

The common assumption of existing paradigms is that modernization is the coherent outcome of the combined and self-reinforcing effects of social and economic development as we have experienced them in the West. This is another way of saying that modernization is perceived as the form of development which makes it possible to evolve an economically dynamic, technologically sophisticated and politically open society. It is accepted that non-Western societies may have different cultural attributes. However, so long as they meet the two criteria of economic success and technological advance they are considered to have modernized.[6] What is puzzling about Africa is the extent to which, unlike most of the rest of the world, it fails on both counts. Does it make sense in such conditions to claim that Africa is modern?

We do not approach the question of modernization from a normative or teleological perspective, seeking to explain why Africa has not followed the same path as other parts of the world. We want instead to make sense of what is happening on the continent from the viewpoint of the logic of those concerned. If Africans believe that being modern is compatible with being 'traditional', then we must understand not just what this means but how it is possible. In so doing, we might well be called upon to consider the possibility that there are different types of modernity, though they might not all be endowed with the same potential for economic and scientific development. Our concern is thus not to dispute existing notions of modernity but merely to assess the texture of Africa's own path to modernization.

Modernity, as we see it, is a dynamic process rather than a state of equilibrium. As such, it is pointless to deem one part of the world categorically modern and another irredeemably traditional. They are simply modern and traditional in different ways. What it is important to distinguish is the instrumental quality of distinct types of modernity. Western modernization has been uniquely effective in combining science and technology with bureaucratic and managerial efficiency, thus establishing the benchmark for what is commonly labelled modern society. East Asia seems today to be in the process of developing its own type of modernity, based on an equally impressive admixture of engineering sophistication and organizational capability.

What is noteworthy about Africa is that modernization has not engendered the same forward movement, in terms of economic progress, as in Europe, America or the Far East. The continent appears to have evolved a form of modernity which provides for the ability

---

[6] Even if, as in some contemporary Asian societies, their record on human rights and individual freedoms is less than impressive.

both to utilize the implements of (social and scientific) Westernization and to remain obdurately 'traditional' in what we would qualify broadly as cultural terms. What is more, there is scarcely any evidence that the use of modern technological instruments has made Westernization more likely. The reverse seems to be true – as though Western modernity was being Africanized.[7]

Our approach thus accounts for a world in which politics is driven by considerations which range from the most decidedly contemporary to the most obviously archaic.[8] What it makes clear is that, far from behaving randomly or irrationally, political actors make sound and shrewd instrumental use of the different registers on which they can legitimately draw. We explain how two complementary logics bind the 'modern' and 'traditional' in Africa today.

The first consists in what we call the re-Africanization of Western concepts or customs according to local socio-cultural norms. We have shown above how this has led to a re-shaping of both political institutions and political actions by more informal and personalized (infra-institutional) African codes of practice. Nevertheless, an interpretation of African politics based on a notion of the hybridization of Western norms is misleading, unless it is made clear that the graft did not have the intended results. To pursue the biological analogy, African genes proved dominant while the imported European ones turned out to be recessive.

The second centres on the ways in which Africans operate simultaneously on what we would describe as different, and largely discrete, registers. We mean here that Africa's political modernity is characterized by a combination of attitudes and habits which draw from a singular fusion of 'modern' and 'traditional' rationalities. We thus emphasize the need to understand the ever changing recourse to the logic of different rational registers, and thereby to explain the extent to which in Africa it is profitable to operate within such a range of 'modern' and 'traditional' approaches.

In the West, societies are organized, regulated and run on principles of instrumental modernity which brook very little dissent. The realm of the traditional is very largely left to individual preferences, desires and beliefs. The modern and traditional do not have the same status. We behave in society on the assumption that we are all in agreement with the rules of modernity which govern our lives. The traditional has no legitimacy in this respect and is of limited practical use in our professional environment. The same is broadly true of the Far East

---

[7] To take but one example, an African academic with an American PhD in psychology will not find it inconsistent to defer to the demands of witchcraft in his village.
[8] African leaders, for example, may well combine the most modern polling techniques with a consultation of their village ancestors (by way of the local medium).

where, cultural differences notwithstanding, societies are similarly regulated.[9]

Such is not the case in Africa. Our point is that on the continent it is both legitimate and advantageous to operate according to different logics of modernity and tradition in all areas of life and work. It is thus not a question of Africans being more 'traditional' (meaning backward) than others. Rather it is the much more pertinent fact that being both traditional and modern is at once justifiable and instrumentally profitable. Having recourse to modern and traditional rationalities, as discussed above, is the norm rather than the exception: it is the reality which any framework of analysis must take into account. We thus need to conceptualize Africa's modernization as embodying a constantly evolving dynamic of apparently disconnected, though in reality overlapping, registers.

Our analytical framework makes it clear why Africa's present modernity encourages the creative use of the 'traditional'. To speak of the traditional in this way, however, is not to imply that our approach is culturalist. Although we give careful attention to the political significance of culture, we do not in any way maintain that politics in Africa is to be explained solely in cultural terms. Our argument is that cultural dynamics, which are most often subsumed under the label of 'tradition', are to be examined from their modern instrumental perspective. Cultural factors are no more and no less important in Africa than they are elsewhere. What is important to our analysis is the way in which such traditions are utilized politically.

The paradigm we have developed shows that what is distinct in Africa is the creative manner in which this overlap of modernity and tradition combines to create a form of political accountability which is rooted in the instrumentalization of disorder. By providing a coherent framework for what might otherwise appear merely as chaos or anarchy, we establish the foundations for an analytical interpretation of politics in Africa which is congruent with classical Weberian approaches.

The meanings of disorder

The foundation of our paradigm is that politics in Africa cannot be understood *sui generis*, in and of itself, divorced from the rest of society, as is the case with a host of other approaches, most notably of the developmentalist ilk. What this means is that analysis must be able to account for events, phenomena and processes which fall outside the

---

[9] Though it is fair to say that, since our notion of the modern is very largely determined by the experience of the West, it is difficult at this stage to know in which ways Asian modernity will eventually differ from that of the West.

usual confines of the discipline of political science. As a result, much of our work has of necessity had to stray on to the grounds of other disciplines, particularly anthropology, sociology and economics. We do not claim to have mastered these disciplines in equal measure. Nor would that have been necessary. Our intention has merely been to investigate their relevance to those areas which we have deemed essential to the comprehension of politics in contemporary Africa.

Our view is that a well-grounded analysis of contemporary Africa must take into account four fundamental aspects of politics on the continent. The first relates to the boundaries of politics. The second has to do with the different registers on which politics is played out. The third concerns the character of rationality evidenced in political action. The last is about the nature of political causality. We discuss each in turn.

(1) The question of boundaries is crucial. If, as we argue here, the limits of the realm of politics are not distinct, then the object of our analysis might itself become uncertain. Where should we look in order to understand the politics of Africa? What is meaningful and what is merely superficial? How do we know? How is it possible to compare the political experience of post-colonial Africa with that of other parts of the world? How, even, do we measure the evolution of one African country against that of another? How, finally, can we tell whether political reforms, such as democratization, are likely to have their intended results?

Our argument is in two parts. The first is that we cannot assume to know what is or is not politically significant in Africa on the basis of any preconceived conceptual framework. The second is that politics in Africa is not functionally differentiated, or separated, from the socio-cultural considerations which govern everyday life. Our method consists in combining the conceptual and the empirical in the following way. We approach the question with universal or classical analytical tools and we attempt to gain enough knowledge of individual African countries to draw conclusions about where it is worthwhile to generalize. It is on this basis that we offer the following observations about the boundaries of politics.

What is remarkable about Africa is the extent to which there is a constant and dynamic interpenetration of the different spheres of human experience: from the political to the religious. All aspects of life appear to affect, immediately and decisively, all others. This makes for a peculiarly difficult analytical situation since, to use a mathematical analogy, all variables are dependent. It is hardly possible, for example, to study voting patterns in national elections as we would in Western societies. Similarly, it is hard to understand the meaning of representation outside an enlarged context which takes into account personal as well as political considerations. Finally, to give a more unconventional example, it is essential to study the influence of the occult on political leadership in order to appreciate the extent to which seemingly political decisions may hinge on what we call the irrational.

The argument that we offer is not so much that everything in Africa may turn out to be political, a generalization often made by those who draw on the French '*politique par le bas*' school of thought, but more subtly, that that which is political may not belong to the overtly recognized political domain. Without a well-considered conceptual approach such as we offer here, the notion that 'low' politics is important can all too easily translate into an argument that there is a significant distinction in this respect between 'low' and 'high' politics. What we would wish to emphasize instead is the extent to which all political actors, from the political elites to the ordinary man and woman, share a common notion of the undifferentiated nature of the political which they all seek to employ profitably.

Our approach makes it clear that it is the very nature of the political instrumentalization of seemingly non-political issues which marks out the political in Africa. The fact that the boundaries of the political are unclear or, more accurately, very porous, only makes the task of understanding the instrumentalization of disorder more complex in practice – though no more difficult conceptually. That is why we have stressed throughout the book the relevance of the informal and of the process of informalization. For us, such informalization is nothing other than the day-to-day instrumentalization of what is a shifting and ill-defined political realm. The question for future analysis is whether in due course that political realm will become more functionally differentiated.

(2) The issue of register is one we have discussed in relation to the question of modernization. We want here more specifically to focus on that aspect which relates to the problem of boundaries as outlined above. Just as the limits of the political are creatively unclear, there is a multiplicity of registers according to which individuals participate politically within society. The first, and most important, point to make in this respect is that African identities are tied to the notion of the individual within the community in ways which defy the conceptualizations most readily offered in the social sciences. Here too, therefore, the boundaries of the notion of the individual are flexible and porous, forcing us thereby to be cosmopolitan in our approach to the political.

The issue of the perception and self-perception of individual identities is indeed fundamental to the workings of any political system. Our understanding of politics is grounded in a number of key assumptions in respect of the definition of the individual and of the relation between citizens and society. In the West, for example, the operation of the political electoral arrangement is supposed to rest on the premise that individuals make decisions on the basis of their distinct opinion and free will. When citizens vote they express a specific personal political preference for a given political programme, however complex the reasoning and influences which have brought about that decision. The very legitimacy of the Western political order derives from the shared belief that individuals can and do make such narrowly circumscribed political decisions. This appears not to be the case in Africa, where the formal notion of the citizen does not correspond to the realities of the link between individual and society.

Our approach thus emphasizes an interpretation of politics in Africa as a mode of operation in which it is both judicious and legitimate to switch from one register to another without undue concern for the political contradictions which such behaviour might appear to induce. The lack of a clear differentiation between various registers, like the lack of distinction about the boundaries of the political, is utilized as a resource by those political actors able to do so. Hence, our notion of disorder is also a reflection of the fuzziness of what constitutes the primary and secondary registers informing politics. Successful political elites in Africa are those which can offer sufficiently meaningful order – that is, both relate and respond to the expectations of their followers. Ultimately, therefore, what marks the political domain is that both elites and the populace share a view of the world that is built upon the overlapping of such different registers.

Although our conceptual discussion may appear somewhat obtuse, examples abound of what we mean concretely. If, for instance, it is true that the place of the occult is central to African life, then it follows that political decisions may be made according to criteria attached to the realm of the beyond, invalidating thereby any analysis that failed to take this factor into account. This does not mean that Africans do not believe in the 'proper' norms of Western political life but simply that they must also take into consideration other aspects of the invisible world which might clash with those Western norms. They thus operate according to two, possibly contradictory, registers.

Similarly, if notions of pride, shame and humiliation are intimately tied with the enunciation of words, then the language of politics will be affected. We are all familiar with the infinite variety of words that are used to refer to the political elites in Africa. We know why all leaders seek a label (chief, lion, big man, etc.) which both makes clear their prominence and roots their position in a vocabulary consonant with notions of 'traditional' legitimacy. We are less sure, however, about the deeper political meanings certain words can have, such as might be attached to witchcraft, the occult or the world of the ancestors. It is clear, however, that such resonances do matter and that they may well affect, directly or indirectly, political processes such as, for example, the current 'democratization'. What word, for example, might be attached to the function of leader of the opposition who, in the real world, has no resources allocated to his position?[10]

Moreover, the very notion that political parties might be considered of equal weight for purposes of democratic elections is one which is often ill-accepted in Africa. This is surely due in part to the fact that parties are more commonly considered as extensions of individual politicians than as impersonal electoral machines whose identities are tied to distinct political programmes. Here too, therefore, it is only possible to understand the relevance of party competition in contemporary Africa by taking into account the many different registers according to which parties are used as political instruments. It is for this reason that parties are rarely what they seem to be – even to genuinely open-minded foreign observers – and why the significance of election results is often obscure, even when a clear winner appears to have emerged. What it is important to understand is that electoral victory may not always determine the legitimacy of the result, as vividly demonstrated by the recent experience of the Congo.

(3) The two aspects of politics discussed above, boundaries and registers, will of necessity affect what we call here the rationality of political action. The assumption in most paradigms is that political rationality is tied to a process of Western modernization. As individuals and societies mature, as the economy develops and as a greater proportion of the population becomes urbanized, so the common argument goes, outlooks and behaviour change. Modernization thus defined brings about the emergence of a type of 'sociological' rationality which is said to mark our own Western societies. It is this sort of rationality that underpins the operation of the modern political order as we know it.

We do not wish here to review the sociology of rationality. Suffice it only to say that even Weber, the father of modern social theory, provided an approach that made it possible to develop an analysis more attuned to the conditions of Africa than most paradigms currently in vogue. Indeed, Weber defined rationality in terms of what individuals and political actors believe for themselves to be rational and not in terms of what outside observers might consider to be the case. Which is another way of saying that what he saw as Western rationality was only what he perceived to have become so in the context of the specific Western socio-economic development of the period. His approach, however, remained open.

---

[10] It is for this reason that co-optation of political opponents is so central to the political life of Africa.

Contemporary observers of Africa, for their part, seem to have lost sight of Weber's method. There is a common assumption that the rise of Western rationality is not just inherently desirable but inevitable. Whatever Africa's history and whatever her development, she too will evolve the norms of Western rationality which are said to characterize Western modernity. The converse of this iron belief in a particular kind of evolutionary process, is that what fails to conform to such rationality must, *ipso facto*, be irrational – that is, not capable of being explained logically. The effects of such a dichotomy in our thinking about the continent have been profound. There is today a greater belief in the 'irrationality' of Africa than there was on the eve of independence, when the departing imperial powers set great store on the preparation of their colonies for self-government.

Two currently highly visible examples will illustrate the point. Western interpretations of ethnicity and violence on the continent almost all concentrate on the sheer irrationality of such fratricidal strife. The bulk of the reports on Rwanda and Liberia, for instance, have concentrated on the extent to which 'age-old tribal hatreds' have fuelled conflicts which have become either genocidal or incomprehensibly 'barbaric'. What is interesting about these explanations of such violence is the fact that they are tied to a notion of the 'backwardness' of Africa. These conflicts occur, it is implied, because Africa has failed to develop the type of Western rationality which would in effect render them obsolete.[11]

Our approach is not premised on such simplifying assumptions. It seeks instead to show that what is happening today in Africa issues from rationalities that are both modern and distinct from what is found in the West. We are guided only by the desire to make sense of what we observe in Africa. And what we observe in Africa suggests to us that the continent is not a cauldron of loose irrationality but an area where distinct types of rationality govern the behaviour of ordinary men and women. This is obviously not to deny that contradictions between distinct registers can be seen as a lack of political coherence – and thus irrational from the modern Western perspective. It is only to point out that such lack of coherence is instrumentalized politically. What we mean by rationality, therefore, is essentially what we can identify as the reasons which impel or convince people to think and behave as they do – what, in other words, provides an analytically coherent explanation for a given political conduct in a given historical context.

To return to the examples given above, it is not analytically satisfactory to suggest that Hutus are killing Tutsis in Rwanda merely because

---

[11] Which, in the light of what has happened in the former Yugoslavia, is a rather strange assumption to make.

they are backward. Nor is it analytically plausible to argue that Taylor is instructing his troops to commit atrocities in Liberia simply because he is a psychopath.[12] We would submit that what has happened in these two countries is both more complex and more universal than is generally recognized. In Rwanda, there has been a succession of identifiable socio-economic crises which have spiralled into political violence and, eventually, degenerated into genocide. In Liberia, the breakdown of the old patrimonial system and Taylor's political ambitions have combined to produce a deadly type of new (and most modern) political violence, which has spilled into neighbouring Sierra Leone, where, if anything, it has become even more vicious.

(4) A discussion of rationality leads us quite naturally to the final element of our approach: namely, the proper consideration of the nature of political causality. Political analysis is, by definition, a search for the most appropriate and most plausible explanation of the causes of given political events and processes. All paradigms offer an interpretation of what political causes have brought about given political consequences. All, therefore, propose a theory of political causality – even if most do so implicitly.

Development theory, for instance, posits that economic growth – that is, growing GDP and the modernization of the economy – will generate a form of political development that is akin to the Western model. Here, it is argued, the institutionalization of political organizations is caused by the processes of social modernization engendered by economic development. For its part, democratization theory assumes that multi-party elections are, *ipso facto*, more likely to bring about Western-style democracy than any other form of electoral process. Hence, multi-party elections are thought in this way 'to cause' democracy – even if it is rarely expressed in such stark form.

The main obstacle we face in attempting to understand contemporary politics on the continent is that, on the face of it, it appears not to conform to the most common political causalities with which we are familiar. Cause and effect are often not what they seem to be. The very words we use to describe politics are often inappropriate. What looks to us, for example, like corrupt ostentation may turn out in reality to embody an element of communal political distinction which we do not recognize. If wealth in part 'causes' political virtue, we need to explain how seemingly illegal forms of enrichment may in fact be taken as justifiable by the members of a particular community. Otherwise we shall fail to understand the political process which brings legitimacy to ostensibly 'corrupt' elites.

---

[12] Psychopaths are more likely to be found among the serial killers which modern society seems to generate with increasing frequency.

Equally, if elections are taken by most to be a form of commerce – votes for goods – it becomes useful to analyse political contests differently from what they may at first appear to represent. Where elections are not seen primarily as a means of registering a preference for a political programme but as an instrument for obtaining material resources, their political significance will be different from that obtaining in Western countries. Electoral contests would have to be understood in terms of material exchange rather than in terms of ideological rationality – or, to use our paradigm, in terms of the political instrumentalization of the uncertainties generated by party competition.

That we should easily be misled in our search for political causalities in Africa is not surprising, given what we have said about boundaries and registers. There is a very powerful sense in which African politicians appear fully to subscribe to the rationality which underlies our own Western political systems. But, and here lies the interpretative difficulty, they also operate on different registers where distinct political causalities apply. It may well in fact be, to return to our earlier example, that elections are seen both in terms of Western rationality and in terms of the instrumentalization of exchange we have suggested. Equally, it may be entirely true that African politicians would both reject corruption in principle and accept in practice that politics has made them rich.

For this reason, ours is not in the least a quest for 'the' political causality most readily to be found on the continent. We try instead to probe political issues with a view to making sense of the multiple (and possibly inconsistent) factors which determine cause and effect, so that, to follow on the same issue, it is very likely that some forms of political enrichment are considered legitimate in some circumstances but not in others.[13] The task of the analyst is to suggest why that is and to make sense of the rationality for such differences, which is what, for example, the notion of the 'criminalization of the state' purports to offer, although in our view such an approach fails to investigate the extent to which what may pass for criminalization is in fact tied up with the notions of legitimacy and political accountability extant in a given national context.[14]

---

[13] Notable examples of illegitimate ostentation would include Houphouët-Boigny's construction in his home town of the largest Catholic cathedral in the world, Mobutu's laying down in his home town of a runway capable of accommodating the Concorde he chartered for his personal use, and Bokassa's coronation as emperor of the Central African Republic.

[14] See Bayart *et al.*, 1998.

The instrumentalization of disorder

The heart of our paradigm is the notion that in contemporary Africa politics turns on the instrumentalization of disorder. The three parts into which the book is divided represent the three areas on which we think it is essential to provide a fresh analysis. This is not to say, as should be obvious to the reader, that we neglect other political considerations or that we deem them of little interest. It is only that we concentrate our efforts on those aspects of socio-economic life which we believe have the most profound political resonance on the continent.

Our interpretation could appear controversial. Indeed, taken literally our view might even seem perverse. How can it seriously be suggested that the political arrangements which govern the lives of such a large number of contemporary nations amount to no more than the exploitation of disorder? Is not modern politics generally to be understood as the construction of political order? Is it not immoderate to imply that Africans should not just resist political order but positively prosper on disorder?

While we recognize these concerns, what we mean is that the disorder of which we speak is in fact a different 'order', the outcome of different rationalities and causalities. It appears as disorder only because most paradigms are based on a notion of a form of social, economic and, therefore, political development which reflects the experience of Western societies. The view that societies could modernize without becoming Westernized is one which most political analysis does not readily entertain. We can still make sense of countries, like those in Asia, that achieve economic success on different cultural bases because at least they are modern in ways which we do understand. But the experience of Africa, where there has been little or no appreciable economic or technological achievement, simply defies our usual notions of order.

Our approach is an attempt to explain how apparent disorder can in fact have its own logic – even if at first that logic seems hardly to contribute to the future prosperity of the continent. Once it is accepted that there are in Africa well-recognized norms of political practice which do not conform to those we find elsewhere, it becomes imperative to predicate our analysis on an interpretative framework which makes sense of those norms. This is what we have sought to accomplish both in the presentation of concepts that can be profitably used and in the development of a political analysis reaching beyond the surface of social, economic and political processes which appear either paradoxical or incomprehensible.

Let us now bring together the various strands of our analysis and present those notions which are most crucial to our paradigm. The point here is not to offer an exhaustive list of all aspects of African life which we consider politically significant but to illustrate the analytical import of our paradigm through a discussion of a judicious selection of key issues in the politics of contemporary Africa. We thus want in the remainder of this chapter successively to touch on: (1) the notion of the individual, (2) the salience of reciprocity, (3) the importance of vertical links, (4) the concept of success, and (5) the imperative of the short-term view and micro-perspective.

(1) We have already discussed at length the notion of the individual. Here we explain how this aspect of social life is relevant to our paradigm. The kernel of our analysis of the concept of identity in sub-Saharan Africa is that individual rationality is essentially based on communal logic. What we mean is twofold. First, individuals act on the whole with a preponderant respect for the psychological, social and religious foundations of the local community from which they are issued. Second, and more generally, relations of power are predicated on the shared belief that the political is communal.

The reverse is usually the case in the West, where the socio-political order is built on the notion that individuals are primarily discrete and very largely self-defined citizens of the nation. This is, of course, a question of emphasis. In the West, individuals are not entirely dissociated from the communal context of social life. Nor are individuals in Africa mere prisoners of their own community, bound by the imperatives of communal logic. On balance, however, there is a fundamental distinction on this question between the two forms of political 'rationality'.

The implications of this communal notion of the individual in Black Africa are both complex and profound. At the very least, it means that we cannot consider the place and role of the individual within the political system as we would do in the West. This may appear a relatively minor point but in some very crucial way it invalidates most existing interpretations of politics in contemporary Africa. Indeed, if we cannot simply assume what individual behaviour may mean politically, as most paradigms do, we have in effect to reconstruct one of the foundation concepts of modern political analysis. We need to conceive of individuals as the nodal points of larger communal networks rather than as single, free and intentional agents.

We can illustrate the importance of this point by reference to one of the latest, and perhaps one of the most sophisticated, studies of political change in present-day Africa.[15] Apposite as the authors' views are on the political-institutional approach best suited to understanding present 'democratic' political transitions on the continent and judicious as their conclusions may be, nowhere in this large volume is

---

[15] Bratton and Van de Walle, 1997.

there any recognition of the pitfalls of conceptualizing individuals as 'citizens'. The notion of citizen is very precisely one which we would take to be Western (or Eurocentric) in that it implies a degree of individual differentiation within society which is almost nowhere to be found in Africa. Moreover, Bratton's and Van de Walle's analysis simply takes for granted that a process of democratization along the present lines will, *ipso facto*, bring about the consolidation of the reality of citizenship, regardless of existing socio-economic conditions.

We would in fact suggest that the reverse is a more likely outcome: democracy might well be Africanized in that the impact of multi-party elections will be seen in a communal rather than an individual framework. In our view, multi-party elections are unlikely to bring about significant change in the nature of individual differentiation in the present context of social, economic and political disorder. We would thus be wary of any suggestion that such transitions might usher in a fundamental mutation in the contemporary political order. The experience of South Africa where, uniquely on the continent, Western and African notions of identity both have deep historical roots, will be an interesting test case of the extent to which Western-style democracy evolves in Africa.

(2) Our conception of the individual leads immediately to a consideration of the importance of the notion of reciprocity, the full significance of which is of great import to the workings of politics in Africa. Our emphasis on this aspect of socio-economic life is due to the observation that political action is in large degree driven by what we might call the imperative of exchange. We do not mean here simply the commerce of reciprocal favours – important as that undoubtedly is in everyday life – which is to be found everywhere in the world, albeit under different guises. We mean instead a more profound notion of what is expected of relations between individuals and the communities which are most relevant to their lives.

What we would say is that, in Africa, the logic of any action (whether political or not) lies in what it induces by way of expectations of reciprocity between the parties involved. Because of the conception of the individual on the continent, relations between people must also be seen as taking into account the communal of which they are a part. This can only be done when there is a clear recognition of the nature of the exchange involved. Relations, as it were, must be propitiated by reciprocity because they are not seen as distinct from the context within which they take place. Thus, political acts are played out on the market place of the various patrimonial networks concerned.

Whereas Western political theory starts from the premise that an individual political act such as voting can be meaningful regardless of the social context within which it is cast, our paradigm makes clear how this context cannot be disregarded in the case of Africa. Any political action is couched in an environment of reciprocity which dictates its symbolic and instrumental value. To return to present political transitions, the process of voting in a multi-party election must be understood as part of (very largely informal) relations of political exchange which impinge directly, if sometimes obscurely, on the electoral result.

For example, it is clear that in many African countries (like Côte d'Ivoire, Mozambique, Senegal or Guinea Bissau) ruling parties were returned to power in part simply because they were perceived to be more able to deliver on expected patrimonial promises than their competitors. Conversely, in other settings (like Zambia, Benin or São Tomé e Príncipe) they were swept from power in part when it was clear that they could no longer deliver. Whatever other considerations may induce voters to prefer one presidential candidate to another, the fact remains that such political support as may be given is expected to bring with it suitable reciprocity: hence, for example, the disillusionment with Frederick Chiluba's austerity measures in Zambia.

(3) That this is the case is, not fortuitously, connected with the third factor we wish to stress: the overriding importance of vertical links within the political system. We know, of course, that such links are the defining features of patrimonial systems. We know too that even Western legal-bureaucratic organizations are not immune to this kind of influence. Our point, however, is rather different. What is significant in Africa is the extent to which vertical and/or personalized, relations actually drive the very logic of the political system. It is not just that politics are swayed by personal considerations or that the personal is manipulated for political reasons. It is also, and perhaps more importantly, that the overall aim of politics is to affect the nature of such personal relations.

What this means is that the ultimate ambition of those who have power is most often to establish their standing as Big Men. Such standing is, by its very nature, subjective and can only be achieved within a context of personalized relations where clients, or dependants, will ensure its recognition. It is not, therefore, sufficient to be acknowledged as the supreme political ruler. It is also necessary to be recognized as the *primus inter pares* among all Big Men, within what Hyden called an economy of affection.[16] The aim of the political elites is not just to gather power. It is much more fundamentally to use that power, and the resources which it can generate, to purchase, as it were, the 'affection' of their people.

---

[16] Hyden, 1980.

Politics is thus about the search for a position of esteem which derives in large part from such subjective factors as status, respect and 'affection'. That is why, for example, the question of corruption in Africa cannot be understood simply within the context of the abuse of power. A well-managed moral economy of corruption does involve the abuse of formal power for personal gains. But, ultimately, personal gains are aimed at achieving a position of legitimate respectability recognized by all. While petty corruption is usually despised by the population at large, because it is merely self-serving and usually arbitrary, there is often a recognition that the elites' much more significant abuse of power serves larger and more legitimate 'moral' purposes.

Our argument here is not to downplay the extent to which personalized relations undermine the very viability of legal and bureaucratic institutionalization – which it most assuredly does. It is, rather, to explain how such personalized relations fit within the more general moral economy of esteem described above. This is not to say that such a moral economy is not itself widely abused by those, like Idi Amin or General Abacha, who sought to remain in power at all costs. Dictators are dictators anywhere in the world and Africa has had more than its fair share of tyrants. It is simply to remind ourselves that we need to be more discriminating in our analytical interpretation of personalized political relations in Africa. Here, as elsewhere, we could do worse than to start with the notion of accountability.[17] People in Africa can tell whether personalized relations are legitimate or not.

A paradoxical consequence of the factors outlined above, particularly in view of the present condition of Africa, is our conviction that a useful paradigm of politics in Africa needs to accommodate the concept of equilibrium. Our argument is that, because there is such a high degree of instability and uncertainty in contemporary Africa, the search for order has led to a strong demand for a state of equilibrium in society. That demand has fuelled a desire to find in existing beliefs and societal values the framework within which some stability could be achieved. In other words, the taming of disorder has heightened what we described in Part II as the 're-traditionalization' of society.

The problem, however, is that development requires the productive use of disequilibrium, meaning here the channelling of the resources generated by inequality into productive investment. There is currently in Africa neither the (technical, social, professional and legal) infrastructure nor, more importantly, the political will to drive development in this way. Consequently, the search for equilibrium takes the form of what we have conceptualized as the political instrumentalization of disorder. The rapid gains reaped by exchange, much of which is now of a 'criminal' nature, are more likely quickly to deliver the

[17] See Chabal, 1992, Chapter 3.

resources needed by the neo-patrimonial system than the long and arduous journey which Western-style economic development entails.

(4) Crucial to the comprehension of current politics on the continent is a notion of what achievement or success means. Development demands, as we know, the kind of productive investment which is most compatible with what Weber identified as the Protestant work ethic. The success of capitalist development is measured in growth, which in turn implies deferred reward. The opposite is the case in Africa. The measure of achievement has long been, and seemingly continues to be, found in the immediate display of material gain – that is, consumption rather than production. At a most fundamental level, then, the logic of the notion of success is antithetical to the economic 'mentality' underpinning development.

There is debate as to why this should be the measure of achievement in Africa.[18] What is cause and what is effect? Do such norms of success only apply because the continent is poor? Would they change if development were initiated successfully or are they themselves one of the main impediments to development? Whatever the most plausible answers to these questions, there is no doubt that at present such norms do apply and that they do have a deleterious effect on Africa's potential for economic development. And, from our observations, there are no indications of a change towards a different set of attitudes.

Ostentation remains, and is likely to remain, one of the chief political virtues in Africa. Or to put it another way, it continues to be more important for political elites to display the right kind of ostentation (including redistributing resources to clients) than to demonstrate the potential achievement of the Protestant work ethic.

From a Western perspective such attitudes exhibit the limits of political ambition in Africa. Few politicians meaningfully engage the population in a discussion of the changes required to achieve a higher rate of growth and more sustained development in the country. Fewer still show by what they do – rather than what they say – that they are even remotely concerned about such issues. There may be talk of development – there have even been in the past development plans – but the reality of the exercise of power does not give much evidence of a commitment to the sort of structural and infrastructural reforms which would make development possible. Oil revenues, for instance, are usually dissipated on conspicuous consumption (such as the construction of a new capital city in Nigeria) and other patrimonial expenses.

Far from becoming less prevalent, the present norm of success seems in practice to be pushing politicians into an ever more frantic search for the means of patrimonial ostentation. The apparently stun-

---

[18] We have reviewed the debate on these issues in Chapter 9.

ning speed with which political liberalization and democratization were embraced (between 1990 and 1994) by the political elites in Africa can, without undue cynicism, be seen in part at least as an attempt to instrumentalize Western political conditionalities for the purpose of making possible the continued, or even increased, delivery of foreign aid which their regimes so desperately require.[19] This concept of achievement entails two further characteristics of politics which we think important: the dominance of the short-term view and the imperative of the micro- (as opposed to macro-) perspective.

(5) These two attributes of modern politics in Africa are easily understood, as they are entirely consistent with the socio-economic norms currently found on the continent. Indeed, the criteria of success identified above make it inevitable that the outlook of the political elites should be both short-term and concerned with the micro- rather than macro-picture of society. The political system (as we have outlined it in Part I) functions in the here and now, not for the sake of a hypothetical tomorrow. It can only work if it meets its obligations continuously. In other words, its legitimacy rests with its immediate achievements, not with its long-term ambitions. It does not allow for delayed reward or achievement – much less for long-term investment.

Similarly, the logic of neo-patrimonialism is focused on the proximate: the local and the communal. Its legitimacy depends on the ability to deliver to those who are linked with the political elites through the micro-networks of patronage and clientelism. There is no scope within such a perspective for deferring to a larger but less immediate macro-rationality, most significantly to the greater good of the country as a whole. Clients will not readily accept sacrifices for more ambitious national goals in a context where it is assumed that patrons only work for their clients. So that the claim by one Big Man that he must reduce expenditures on his clients because resources are needed for national development would not normally be credible or acceptable.

By stressing what we take to be two powerful political imperatives, we do not thereby mean to imply that other factors are not at work. Because political elites operate on a number of different registers – both modern and 'traditional' – the analysis of politics in Africa needs to take into account the ways in which those registers impinge on political outcomes. It is obvious that politicians will try to maximize the effect of their action in terms which are not limited to the short-term and micro-perspective. They quite naturally want to be seen to succeed in the modern developmentalist ambitions which are at the centre of their political ideology. They will, accordingly, rationalize

[19] As we have shown in Chapter 8.

what they do by means of a discourse which will omit to highlight the considerations we have stressed.

Some, like Nyerere or Museveni, may well have a relatively modest personal need for the status of Big Man and may genuinely aim to transcend the short-term view in favour of longer-term developmental goals. A few, like Nelson Mandela, may in fact embody the highest virtues of the Protestant work ethic.[20] The fact remains, however, that the ability of such exceptional leaders to move the political system beyond its present rationality is limited, not primarily because of a lack of ambition but much more fundamentally because of the nature of existing forms of political legitimacy. In the end, there is an interlocking neo-patrimonial logic between the deep ambitions of the political elites and the well-grounded expectations of their clients.

* * *

Our (admittedly far from cheering) conclusion is that there prevails in Africa a system of politics inimical to development as it is usually understood in the West. The dynamics of the political instrumentalization of disorder are such as to limit the scope for reform in at least two ways. The first is that, where disorder has become a resource, there is no incentive to work for a more institutionalized ordering of society. The second is that in the absence of any other viable way of obtaining the means needed to sustain neo-patrimonialism, there is inevitably a tendency to link politics to realms of increased disorder, be it war or crime. There is therefore an inbuilt bias in favour of greater disorder and against the formation of the Western-style legal, administrative and institutional foundations required for development.

Consequently, the prospects for political institutionalization are, in our view, limited. Nor is it likely that the recent democratic experiments in Africa will lead to the establishment of the constitutional, legal and bureaucratic political order which is required for fundamental reform. Such change would have to be driven by popular will. Only when ordinary African men and women have cause to reject the logic of personalized politics, seriously to question the legitimacy of the present political instrumentalization of disorder and to struggle for new forms of political accountability, will meaningful change occur. Tempting as it is to think that political liberalization, the so-called democratization of Africa, will facilitate such change, there is in the

---

[20] The paradigm we present is, in our view, not necessarily applicable to South Africa, which we believe to be structurally different from the rest of Black Africa because of its distinct historical experience.

foreseeable future little likelihood that it will. We simply cannot know how Africa will evolve politically.

Our paradigm offers a method for understanding the present condition of Africa which is neither normative nor teleological. Its analytical import is to make it possible to explain how it is that Africa 'works' in the absence of proper political institutionalization or sustained economic development. We do not present solutions to the problems of Africa, merely a diagnosis of its predicament. That is why it is worth stating again that our argument cannot be used as evidence to support the view either that Africans are 'inherently' different from us or that they are 'inherently' incapable of changing the condition of the countries in which they live. Nor can it remotely be construed as condoning what is happening on the continent today. As Africanists we can only deplore the consequences of the present economic, social and political crisis. As political analysts we can do no more than offer what we believe to be a well-considered appraisal of that crisis.

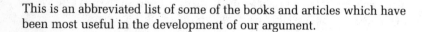

This is an abbreviated list of some of the books and articles which have been most useful in the development of our argument.

Anderson, B., 1983, *Imagined Communities*. London: New Left.
Austen, R., 1987, *African Economic History*. London: James Currey.
Badie, B., 1992, *L'Etat importé: l'occidentalisation de l'ordre politique*. Paris: Fayard.
Badie, B. and Birnbaum, P., 1979, *Sociologie de l'Etat*. Paris: Grasset (English version: Chicago University Press).
Bailey, F.G., 1980, *Stratagems and Spoils: A social anthropology of politics*. Oxford: Basil Blackwell.
Balandier, G., 1957, *Afrique ambiguë*. Paris: Plon.
Bayart, J.-F., Ellis, S. and Hibou, B., 1998, *The Criminalization of the State in Africa*. Oxford: James Currey for the International African Institute.
Berman, B. and Lonsdale, J., 1992, *Unhappy Valley: Conflict in Kenya and Africa*. London: James Currey.
Bourdieu, P., 1980, *Le Sens pratique*. Paris: Editions de Minuit.
Bourmaud, D., 1997, *La politique en Afrique*. Paris: Montchrestien.
Bratton, M. and Van de Walle, N., 1997, *Democratic Experiments in Africa: regime transitions in comparative perspective*. Cambridge and New York: Cambridge University Press.
Callaghy, T.M., 1984, *The State-Society Struggle*. New York: Columbia University Press.
Callaghy, T.M., 1994, 'Civil society, democracy, and economic change in Africa: a dissenting opinion about resurgent societies', in J. Harbeson, D. Rothchild and N. Chazan (eds), *Civil Society and the State in Africa*. Boulder, CO: Lynne Rienner.
Chabal, P., (ed.) 1986, *Political Domination in Africa*. Cambridge: Cambridge University Press.
Chabal, P., 1992, 1994, *Power in Africa: an essay in political interpretation*. Basingstoke: Macmillan.
Chabal, P., 1996, 'The African crisis: context and interpretation', in R. Werbner and T. Ranger (eds), *Postcolonial Identities in Africa*. London: Zed Press.
Chabal, P., 1997, 'Apocalypse Now? A post-colonial journey into Africa'. An inaugural lecture. London: King's College London.
Chazan, N. *et al.*, 1988, *Politics and Society in Contemporary Africa*. London: Macmillan.

Chrétien, J.-P. and Prunier, G. (eds), 1989, *Les ethnies ont une histoire*. Paris: Karthala.

Clapham, C., 1996, *Africa and the International System: the politics of state survival*. Cambridge: Cambridge University Press.

Constantin, F. and Coulon, C., 1997, (eds), *Religion et transition démocratique en Afrique*. Paris: Karthala.

Coquery-Vidrovitch, C., 1985, *Afrique noire, permanences et ruptures*. Paris: Payot. (English version: University of California Press, 1988).

Cruise O'Brien, C., *et al*. (1989), *Contemporary West African States*. Cambridge: Cambridge University Press.

Daloz, J.-P., 1996, 'Les ambivalences dans la caricature des dirigeants politiques: illustrations africaines', *Mots* (Paris), 48 (September).

Daloz, J.-P. (ed.), 1998, *Le (non) renouvellement des élites en Afrique subsaharienne*. Paris: Economica.

Daloz, J.-P. and Chileshe, J.D., 1996 (eds), *La Zambie contemporaine*. Paris: IFRA/Karthala.

Daloz, J.-P. and Quantin, P. (eds), 1997, *Transitions démocràtiques africaines: dynamiques et contraintes (1990–1994)*. Paris: Karthala.

Diamond, L. (ed.), 1993, *Political Culture and Democracy in Developing Countries*. Boulder, CO: Lynne Rienner.

Dunn, J., 1979, *Western Political Theory in the Face of the Future*. Cambridge: Cambridge University Press.

Eisenstadt, S., 1972, *Traditional Patrimonialism and Modern Neopatrimonialism*. London: Sage.

Ekeh, P. P., 1990, 'Social Anthropology and Two Contrasting Uses of Tribalism', *Comparative Studies of Society and History*, 32 (4).

Fardon, R., 1996, 'Destins croisés': histoire des identités ethniques et nationales en Afrique de l'Ouest', *Politique Africaine*, 61 (March).

Gellner, E., 1983, *Nations and Nationalism*. Oxford: Blackwell.

Geschiere, P., 1995, *Sorcellerie et politique en Afrique: la viande des autres*. Paris: Karthala.

Geschiere, P., 1996, 'Sorcellerie et politique: les pièges du rapport élite-village', *Politique Africaine*, 63 (October).

Geertz, C., 1973, *The Interpretations of Cultures*. New York: Basic books.

ter Haar, G., 1992, *Spirit of Africa: the healing ministry of Archbishop Milingo of Zambia*. London: Hurst.

Hobsbawm, E. and Ranger, T., 1983, *The Invention of Tradition*. Cambridge: Cambridge University Press.

Huntington, S.P., 1991 *The Third Wave: democratization in the late twentieth century*. Norman, OK: University of Oklahoma Press.

Hyden, G., 1980, *Beyond Ujamaa in Tanzania*. London: Heinemann.

Iliffe, J., 1987, *The African Poor*. Cambridge: Cambridge University Press.

Jackson, R. and Roseberg, C., 1982, *Personal Rule in Black Africa*. Berkeley, CA: University of California Press.

Joseph, R., 1987, *Democracy and Prebendal Politics in Nigeria*. Cambridge: Cambridge University Press.

Kabou, A., 1991, *Et si l'Afrique refusait le développement?* Paris: L'Harmattan.

Lonsdale, J., 1989, 'Africa's Pasts in Africa's Future', *Canadian Journal of African Studies*, 23/1.

Lonsdale, J., 1996, 'Ethnicité morale et tribalisme politique', *Politique Africaine*, 61 (March).

Martin, D.C., 1988, *Tanzanie, l'invention d'une culture politique*. Paris: FNSP/Karthala.

Médard, J.-F., 1982, 'The underdeveloped state in tropical Africa: political clientelism or neo-patrimonialism?'. in C. Clapham (ed.), *Private Patronage and Public Power: political clientelism in the modern state*. London: Frances Pinter.

Médard, J.-F. (ed.), 1991, *Etats d'Afrique noire: Formations, mécanismes et crises.* Paris: Karthala.

Médard, J.-F, 1992, 'Le 'Big Man' en Afrique: esquisse d'analyse du politicien entrepreneur', *L'Année sociologique* (Paris).

Migdal, J., 1988, *Strong Societies and Weak States: state-society relations and state capabilities in the third world.* Princeton, NJ: Princeton University Press.

Mudimbe, V., 1988, *The Invention of Africa.* Bloomington, IN: Indiana University Press.

Nicolas, G., 1986, *Don rituel et échange marchand dans une société sahélienne.* Paris: Institut d'Ethnologie.

Nicolas, G., 1987, 'Les nations à polarisation variable et leur Etat: le cas nigérien', in E. Terray (ed.), *L'Etat contemporain en Afrique.* Paris: L'Harmattan.

Olivier de Sardan, J.-P., 1996, 'L'économie morale de la corruption en Afrique', *Politique africaine*, 63 (October).

Oyugi, W. *et al.*, 1988, *Democratic Theory and Practice in Africa.* London: James Currey.

Prunier, G., 1995, *The Rwanda Crisis: history of a genocide, 1959–1994.* London: Hurst.

Quantin, P. (ed.), 1994, *L'Afrique politique 1994: vue sur la démocratisation à marée basse.* Paris/Talence: Karthala/CEAN.

Reno, W., 1995, *Corruption and State Politics in Sierra Leone.* Cambridge: Cambridge University Press.

Richards, P., 1996, *Fighting for the Rain Forest: war, youth and resources in Sierra Leone.* Oxford: James Currey for the International African Institute.

Richards, P., 1998, 'Sur la nouvelle violence politique en Afrique: le sectarisme séculier en Sierra Leone', Politique Africaine, 70 (June).

Rothchild, D. and Olorunsola, V.A., 1982, (eds), *State versus Ethnic Claims: African policy dilemmas.* Boulder, CO: Westview Press.

Saro-Wiwa, K., 1991, *Similia: Essays on Anomic Nigeria.* London/Lagos: Saros International.

Schatzberg, M.G., 1988, *The Dialectics of Oppression in Zaire.* Bloomington, IN: Indiana University Press.

Schatzberg, M.G., 1993, 'Power, Legitimacy and "Democratization" in Africa', *Africa*, 63.

Sklar, R., 1986, 'Democracy in Africa.' in Chabal, P. (ed.) 1986.

Soyinka, W., 1996, *The Open Sore of a Continent: a personal narrative of the Nigerian crisis.* Oxford: Oxford University Press.

Terray, E., 1986, 'Le climatiseur et la véranda'. in *Afrique plurielle, Afrique actuelle: Hommage à Georges Balandier.* Paris: Karthala.

Theobald, R., 1990, *Corruption, Development and Underdevelopment.* Basingstoke: Macmillan.

de Waal, A., 1997, *Famine Crimes.* Oxford: James Currey for the International African Institute.

White, G., 1996, 'Civil society, democratization and development', in R. Luckham and G. White (eds), *Democratization in the South: The Jagged Wave.* Manchester: Manchester University Press.

Willame, J.-C., 1995, 'Un autre regard sur la conflictualité politique au Zaïre ', *Politique africaine*, 60 (December).

Young, C., 1982, *Ideology and Development.* New Haven, CT: Yale University Press.

Young, C., 1994, *The African Colonial State in Comparative Perspective.* New Haven, CT: Yale University Press.

INDEX

This index does not include the names of authors cited in the book, with the exception of a few prominent past scholars – Weber, Lévi-Bruhl, Schumpeter, etc.